The Weaning GP

A doctor's guide to feeding your baby

Dr SARIKA DEWAN

Contents

Introduction 4

PART ONE

The Principles of Weaning 9

What is Weaning 10
When to Start 12
How to Wean 20
Building a Balanced Meal 27
Things to Watch Out for 44
Navigating Allergies 53

Getting Started 65

Equipment You'll Need 66
Weaning in Practice 70
How to Introduce Allergens 84
Getting Used to Mealtimes 88
How and When to Transition to Cow's Milk 98
Food Safety and Storage 100
Handling Setbacks 102
Managing Your Own Anxieties 110
Weaning Principles 116

PART TWO

Transition Meals *122*

Breakfast *140*

Lunch *164*

Dinner *186*

Puddings *210*

Snacks and Dips *224*

Conversion tables 248
Further resources 250
Endnotes 251
Acknowledgements 252
Index 253
About the Author 255

The information in this book has been compiled by way of general guidance in relation to the specific subjects addressed but is not a substitute and not to be relied on for medical, healthcare, pharmaceutical or other professional advice on specific circumstances and in specific locations. Please consult your GP before changing, stopping or starting any medical treatment. So far as the author is aware the information given is correct and up to date as at March 2025. Practice, laws and regulations all change, and the reader should obtain up-to-date professional advice on any such issues. The author and publishers disclaim, as far as the law allows, any liability arising directly or indirectly from the use, or misuse, of the information contained in this book.

Introduction

Starting solids is such an exciting time for you and your baby, but you might be wondering how your baby will suddenly learn to eat food. When should you start? What foods should you prepare? How much should you offer? Which feeding method should you choose? I have written this book to answer all those questions and more while trying to keep it as easy and simple as possible. As an NHS GP and often sleep-deprived mother of two, I know that weaning can feel like a bit of a daunting task.

I encountered multiple challenges when weaning my first baby and struggled to find evidence-based, practical resources in one place to guide me. So, to alleviate my anxiety and rebuild my confidence, I researched everything I possibly could about weaning. Combined with my existing medical experience, this allowed me to fully embrace the weaning journey and I am now passionate about passing on that knowledge to other parents/caregivers. As 'The Weaning GP' on Instagram, it is my mission to spread the word and, in this book, I hope to provide a reassuring voice throughout your weaning journey so you can feel confident, which will, in turn, help your little one to feel confident with solids too.

Every baby will have their own unique weaning journey and there will be inevitable ups and downs along the way. However, if you have access to the right information, you can approach weaning with confidence and feel empowered to make the right decisions for you and your family to ensure a smooth transition from milk to a varied solid diet. During the highs, I want you to thoroughly enjoy and hold on to those precious moments with your baby. During the lows, I want you to feel like you're not alone in this and have a resource at your fingertips to refer back to.

At the start of your journey, I recommend breaking things down into smaller steps and thinking one week at a time, or even one day at a time, to help ease yourself in and prevent overwhelm. Throughout this book, you will find up-to-date guidance, handy tips, breakout boxes and simple diagrams to help make things as easy to understand as possible. This means your brain can do less of the thinking and more of the being fully present to enjoy this new and exciting experience with your baby!

PART 1

Part One of this book serves as your essential weaning guide, covering everything you need to know about transitioning from milk to solids. It will take you through every step of the journey, right from the signs that your baby is ready to wean to getting started and progressing through different textures and finger foods.

It is divided into two chapters – the first focuses on the principles of weaning to help you decide how, what and when to wean. It also includes a comprehensive section on navigating allergies. The second chapter focuses on the practical aspects of weaning such as equipment, sample routines, food preparation and storage, and handling common setbacks that many parents encounter.

This is everything I would have wanted to know as a first-time and second-time mum when starting solids, and it has also been reviewed by trusted experts in the field to ensure it is up to date. I sincerely hope it is a helpful and enjoyable read!

The Principles of Weaning

CHAPTER 1

In this chapter, I will be covering the basics of weaning and everything you need to know before you offer your baby their first bite of food. This includes the theory behind why we wean, how your baby naturally prepares for weaning and how to spot when they are ready. I will also touch on when to seek professional help as this is a grey area for many parents/caregivers. There is also information on putting together nutritious, balanced meals, which can take up a lot of brain space for sleep-deprived parents/caregivers, and advice on following a plant-based/vegetarian diet. If you are in two minds about which way to wean, don't worry – I have outlined all the benefits and drawbacks of the different methods to allow you to decide what works best for you as a family. It's a very personal decision and there is by no means one perfect approach!

Once you have started weaning, there are some key areas that are helpful to focus on to make the journey safer for your little one, such as foods to avoid, preparing foods safely, choking hazards, how to spot gagging versus choking and when to intervene. We'll explore all this too so you know what to do should a rare emergency arise.

Given the huge increase we are seeing in the number of allergies, the difficulties in getting a diagnosis and the help needed to manage them, I was also very keen to include a comprehensive section on navigating allergies such as how to recognise them, what to do, how to move forward with your doctor and ensure your child receives the care they need by advocating for them.

As you can see, there is a lot to cover, but I've tried to make it as straightforward and simple as possible to boost your confidence when starting on this journey with your little one.

Let's get started with a question I hear so many times from parents/caregivers: what exactly *is* weaning?

What Is Weaning?

Weaning is the gradual introduction of solid food into your baby's diet as they transition from exclusively drinking milk to eating the same food as the rest of the family. This process tends to start at around six months and continues over several months while your baby develops their feeding skills. At the start, don't worry about how much your baby is eating. It is more about getting them used to the idea of eating as most of their energy and nutrients will still be coming from breast milk or infant formula. The main aim in the early days is to expose your baby to a wide range of flavours and textures to positively influence their feeding skills and taste preferences, while still allowing them to progress at their own pace. Weaning helps children to develop fine motor skills, hand–eye coordination and independence, while enjoying a wide variety of foods ensures they obtain the nutrients they need for growth, brain development and a healthy immune system.

'Weaning' in this context does not mean stopping breast milk or infant formula. As solid food is offered in addition to milk, weaning is also known as 'complementary feeding'. Breast milk or infant formula still provide most of your baby's nourishment up until the age of 12 months. The World Health Organization (WHO) recommends breastfeeding until the age of two years or longer. If you choose not to breastfeed, or are unable to, infant formula is the best equivalent. It should be used as your baby's main milk until at least 12 months, and sometimes longer in specific circumstances such as milk allergy. We'll explore more about milk on page 26.

Why do we wean?

There are three main reasons why we start our babies on solid food:

1. Solid food is necessary to meet the nutritional needs of your rapidly growing baby, which can no longer be met by milk alone. Their own nutrient stores (e.g. iron) start to become depleted at around six months.
2. There is a window of opportunity for babies to become exposed to different textures and flavours and this is thought to help increase variety in their diet in later life.
3. It helps them to practise key developmental skills, such as improving coordination and offers frequent opportunities for social interaction and language learning.

Family mealtimes are a great time for connection, conversation and role-modelling behaviour. Establishing structured and predictable mealtimes can provide your little one with an important sense of security and stability.

THE PRINCIPLES OF WEANING

When to Start

There has been some controversy around when to start babies on solids and research continues to develop in this area. Let's take a look at how things have changed over recent years.

In 2001, the WHO recommended that babies were exclusively breastfed for the first six months of their lives based on a review of several large studies conducted worldwide. In 2003, the UK Department of Health also adopted this policy. Prior to 2001, it was recommended that weaning began from four months, which is why there still may be some confusion if you ask your parents or grandparents for weaning advice.

The WHO continues to recommend starting solids at around six months old as breast milk is the best source of nutrition until this time. It is thought to be the safest time for babies, particularly with concerns over food hygiene and nutrition in developing countries. There are also some key nutrients which become difficult to obtain from milk alone at around six months, such as iron and zinc.

How your baby naturally prepares for weaning

A baby is not born ready to digest solid foods – their bodies still have a little more developing to do. It is fascinating how these natural processes are happening in the background as our babies grow to help get them ready for starting solids. This is another reason why it is so important to wait until babies are physiologically ready for solids (at around six months).
There are specific milestones that your baby will reach to help them safely and efficiently consume solid foods.

Around 4-6 months

GOOD HEAD AND NECK CONTROL
This helps to stabilise babies in an upright position and allows them to safely swallow solids.

LOSS OF TONGUE-THRUST (EXTRUSION) REFLEX
This reflex causes babies to push solid objects out of their mouths. It lessens over time allowing babies to accept and swallow solids.

THE PRINCIPLES OF WEANING

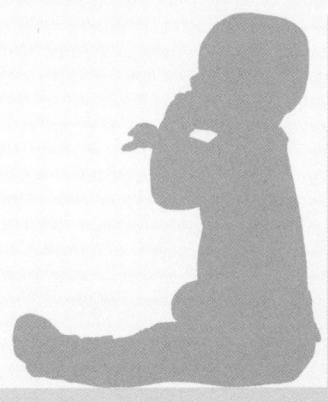

Around 8-10 months

DEVELOPMENT OF PINCER GRASP
Another essential milestone allowing babies to self-feed by picking up small pieces of food with their thumb and forefinger.

Around 6-9 months

DEVELOPMENT OF MUNCHING AND CHEWING MOVEMENTS
Babies start to develop the ability to move solid foods around their mouths and chew them – a skill needed for consumption.

Around 6-8 months

ABILITY TO SIT UPRIGHT
Sitting upright (with or without support) is one of the most fundamental milestones for introducing solids as it reduces the risk of choking.

INCREASED INTEREST IN FOOD
Babies will carefully watch others eat and try to reach for their food which may also suggest readiness for solids.

THE PRINCIPLES OF WEANING

There are also some ongoing developments in your baby's digestive system and oral-motor skills that help to prepare them for solid foods:

DIGESTIVE ENZYMES INCREASE: 	At birth, the enzyme lactase breaks down lactose in milk, but when solids are introduced, more enzymes are produced to break down food.
SALIVARY GLANDS DEVELOP:	As time progresses, more saliva is produced and salivary enzymes break down food when chewing.
STOMACH STARTS TO PRODUCE ACID:	As the stomach lining matures, more acid is produced to help fight germs and break down food such as protein.
GUT MATURES: 	The intestines continue to adapt in shape and size to maximise nutrient absorption.
DIVERSITY INCREASES IN THE GUT MICROBIOME:	Good bacteria start to colonise the gut and the diversity increases as solid food is introduced.
INTESTINAL MUSCLES DEVELOP:	The muscles of the intestine become more coordinated and efficient at moving food through the digestive system.
DEVELOPMENT OF ORAL-MOTOR SKILLS: 	Babies continue to develop control over their lips, tongue and jaw muscles, helping them to coordinate moving food around and swallowing.

Signs of readiness

I always recommend looking out for signs of readiness to help you decide when to start weaning as opposed to focusing on an exact date or age. If your baby is showing all the signs listed below a couple of weeks before turning six months, then go ahead and give it a go – both of my babies started at five-and-a-half months for this reason as they were early sitters. Equally, you may start solids at six months to the day and realise your baby isn't ready at all, in which case it's perfectly OK to stop and wait a week or so before trying again rather than making it an unpleasant experience for you both. It's so easy to get caught up in comparing your baby with others who are of a similar age and may have already started weaning or are eating more than yours, but please try not to worry about what other parents are doing. Learning to eat is a marathon not a sprint, and babies who are the same age won't necessarily be developmentally ready at the same stage. You as a parent may also not feel physically or psychologically ready, so stick to your gut instinct on this, knowing that most babies will be ready at around six months.

You must never feed your baby solids before four months (seventeen weeks old)

According to current guidelines, your baby may be ready to start weaning if they can:
- stay in a sitting position, holding their head steady (sitting does not need to be fully independent and can be supported with a cushion as long as it can be maintained)
- coordinate their eyes, hands and mouth so they can look at their food, pick it up and put it in their mouth
- swallow food (rather than spit it back out)

Babies may also start to show interest in food and watching you eat, so it can be helpful to include them at the dinner table during mealtimes so they can watch and learn. They do not necessarily need to be in a highchair – they can simply watch you while sitting on your lap or in a bouncer.

Signs that are often mistaken for baby being ready for solids include:
- chewing fists
- wanting extra milk feeds
- waking up in the night (more than usual)
- first teeth coming through
- reaching a particular weight
- refusing to breastfeed

These behaviours can be a normal part of your baby's development and are not necessarily signs your baby is ready to start solids. Although starting solids can improve sleep for some babies, it can also worsen sleep for others, so I wouldn't recommend starting based on your baby waking up more frequently at night. Typically, my eldest's sleep hugely improved with solids; however, my youngest's got much worse, so there really is no way to predict how your baby will respond!

You may walk down the supermarket aisle and see lots of baby cereals and snacks marketed for babies from four months onwards. However, it is really important to follow the guidance and start solids only when your baby is showing the signs of readiness outlined above. Many of these finger food snacks are not particularly nutrient-dense and, at this stage, every bite counts as babies only have little stomachs. While these foods can be great for your baby to practise holding finger foods and develop hand–eye coordination, we don't want to be displacing nutritious milk or whole foods with them. While some baby cereals are fortified and can be a good choice, these expensive options are not essential to weaning your baby and their first food does not have to be baby rice or porridge, unless you want it to be. (See page 71 for more on first tastes.)

Multiple babies

If you have twins, triplets or more, it can be a little tricky deciding when to wean your babies. It is just as important to wait for the signs of readiness listed above and it is quite common for one baby to be ready before another. This means you may choose to start weaning one baby and freeze leftover food for the other child/children for when they are ready. If you are starting at the same time, it may be easier to use one bowl and one spoon for all babies and try to ensure you have everything at your fingertips, such as wipes, to make it easier. It is always worth thinking about where you will put the non-weaning baby(s) safely while you focus on the weaning baby in their highchair.

When to seek professional help

There are several circumstances which may require professional advice when transitioning your baby from milk to solid foods. Some babies with specific medical conditions may not show signs of readiness at the expected time (around six months). If you have any worries, especially as a first-time parent/caregiver, I highly recommend discussing them as early as you can with the relevant healthcare professional. It will also help you to understand what to expect for your baby's individual circumstances and reassure you before starting.

It is impossible to cover them all in detail here but below is a short list of scenarios that should prompt a visit to your family doctor or paediatric team before weaning begins:

- Prematurity (babies born before 37 weeks)
- Faltering growth (see page 105)
- Genetic differences (e.g. trisomy 21)
- Metabolic disorders (e.g. phenylketonuria)
- Anatomical differences (e.g. craniofacial abnormalities)
- Neurological conditions/developmental delay (e.g. cerebral palsy)
- Any other medical condition (e.g. food allergies – see page 53)

With many of these conditions, there is often a wide spectrum and there may be some babies who are able to wean as any other child would with minimal input. The professional advice may be to carry on as normal. However, in many of these cases, it is essential to work closely with a multi-disciplinary team consisting of a paediatric doctor, a paediatric dietitian, a speech and language therapist, an occupational therapist, a physiotherapist and, in some cases, a clinical nurse specialist to develop an individualised plan for starting solids.

The management plan will need to consider your baby's developmental needs and nutritional requirements while prioritising their safety when eating and also their growth. Once a plan is made, your child will be reviewed according to their needs and progress with the appropriate adjustments in place.

Developmental milestones

Developmental milestones are things that most children can do by a certain age. Most children will develop every day in terms of movement, language, learning, emotions and behaviour. The timing will vary with each child, but milestones can help us to recognise if there is a delay in any area. As the milestones are based on 'most' not 'all' children, some children who appear 'delayed' may simply need a little more time to practise without there being any cause for concern. If you are worried about your child's development, particularly if they are not reaching multiple milestones, then it is worth a chat with your health visitor or family doctor. Following an assessment of your baby, any necessary referrals and early support can be arranged as needed.

How to Wean

Let's now get stuck into the practical aspects of how you are going to introduce solids to your baby and look at the benefits and drawbacks you may want to consider before making a decision.

Broadly speaking, there are three different approaches you can take to weaning, varying from spoon-feeding, baby-led weaning or a combination of both. Research has found benefits to all of these approaches, but there is currently no universally agreed 'best' way to wean. This is because a lot of the research that has been carried out consists of relatively small numbers of babies and is difficult to generalise to the whole population. There are so many factors that influence how a baby will take to solid foods and what their future eating habits will look like, which can be hard to control or account for in these studies.

The approach you take is a personal decision and what may work for some families won't work for others. There will also be elements of cultural variation, so it is best to choose what feels right for you and your baby after weighing up all the information. Here we will look at the different methods and possible benefits and drawbacks to help you to make an informed decision.

Spoon-feeding

Traditionally, this involves feeding your baby by bringing a spoon to their mouth. Usually, it will be some sort of puréed food offered and babies have very little control over the process. Babies will gradually transition from smooth to lumpy to mashed and then chopped foods, moving at a manageable pace. All babies are different and some might be eating chopped food at seven months, while others won't be ready until nine months. As always, it's important to follow your baby's cues and signals, and do what feels right for your family.

BENEFITS of spoon-feeding

- Far less messy as food is controlled on the spoon.

- Quicker and potentially more flexible for some families who may be in a rush.

- Baby tends to consume more food, particularly in the early stages which *may* be seen as a benefit.

- It's a gradual approach to solids so parents/caregivers may feel more confident about it.

- May lead to less food waste as food can't necessarily be thrown on the floor.

DRAWBACKS of spoon-feeding

- Baby is reliant on you to eat and so you are not able to eat your food at the same time.

- Food needs to be specially prepared – for example, puréed – which may take more time, or you may end up spending more on baby-specific foods or pouches.

- Oral-motor skills may not develop as quickly, which may make it harder for your baby to handle finger food or textured food further down the line.

- Can be easier to overfeed with purées and displace milk too quickly.

- Baby is traditionally not in control, so *may* impact self-regulation of food and intuitive eating as weaning progresses.

Baby-led weaning

Baby-led weaning has become increasingly popular over recent years and is about offering your baby a selection of finger foods and allowing them to explore, pick up and be in control of what they eat. Often, the purée step is completely missed out and families will offer what they are eating with small adjustments to make it safe right from the first days of weaning. Many feel this is may be going back to how children were naturally fed before the arrival of the baby food industry.

BENEFITS
of baby-led weaning

- Baby is in control of what they eat and their appetite.

- Baby is simply eating what the family eats with no specially prepared foods or purées.

- Self-feeding encourages the development of oral-motor skills more quickly.

- Baby *may* be exposed to a wider variety of textures and flavours, which can be linked to reduced fussy eating later in life (this is not guaranteed and research is ongoing).

DRAWBACKS
of baby-led weaning

- Tends to be the messiest approach of them all.

- May lead to excessive food waste with lots of food being squished/thrown on the floor.

- Difficult to tell how much baby is consuming – likely to be less initially than if spoon-feeding purées, which can cause worry over nutrient intake.

- Baby is likely to gag more which can be distressing for parents/caregivers and sometimes lead to vomiting if excessive. (The current evidence does not show an increased risk of choking with baby-led weaning.)

Combination feeding

This is a combination of offering finger foods and spoon-feeding while being guided by your baby as to which they prefer. Starting this way may help you and your baby to develop confidence with weaning initially with spoon-feeding before adding in finger foods to obtain the benefits of both methods.

BENEFITS of combination feeding	DRAWBACKS of combination feeding
• Combining both baby-led weaning and spoon-feeding may help to give flexibility on a particular day and reduce stress levels.	• It can still be very messy and you still have to sit and load the spoon, so it can feel like you are not getting either the benefit of being able to 'leave them to it' or 'be in control of mess'.
• If your baby is not taking to finger food initially, spoon-feeding can help them still consume some solids to meet their nutrient needs. You are still giving your baby some element of independence with the finger food and allowing them to practise their oral-motor skills when they are eating finger foods.	• The risk of overfeeding with spoon-feeding remains as your baby may not have the time to register they are full, which can result in a drop in milk feeds too quickly.
• It can help to give your baby autonomy from the get-go as you are offering both options and are allowing them to choose how they want to eat. This is likely to reduce mealtime stress as they have an element of control.	• It may still lead to food waste, with finger foods being squashed or thrown on the floor.
• Your baby can still be exposed to a wide variety of textures and flavours while practising both methods.	

You can still spoon-feed your baby in a 'baby-led' fashion by pre-loading the spoon with food and offering it to your little one to place to their mouths. This may also help you to read their cues when they have finished the meal as they may stop taking the spoon or drop it (see pages 73–74 for more on hunger/fullness cues and responsive feeding).

How to choose?

If you listen to friends, family or social media, many will have differing opinions on how to wean, and it can be easy to lose confidence or constantly feel like you are doing things the 'wrong' way. We know that how you feel can be sensed by your baby, so my advice is to choose the method you believe in and that makes sense to you so you can feel calm, relaxed and confident during this journey – which will, in turn, help your baby to feel confident too.

The most important thing is to expose your baby to a wide variety of flavours and textures whichever approach you take. Finger food should be introduced at the earliest opportunity and ideally by eight months if choosing to spoon-feed, to help your baby develop key oral-motor skills at a time when they are most adaptable. If your baby suffers with a medical condition, then you may be given specific individual advice on which approach to take when weaning your baby (refer back to page 17 for advice on specific conditions).

On a personal note, I found combination feeding was the best way to wean both of my babies. It allowed me to offer both options and follow my babies' lead on what they preferred. With my firstborn, he very quickly showed a preference for eating with his hands and it became difficult to offer a spoon past seven months. He was adept at picking up food and would shovel it in very quickly, which was great for consumption; however, it often led to overstuffing and lots of gagging, which made me anxious at times. On the other hand, my second born wasn't initially impressed with finger food and would often throw it or squish it. She loved to self-feed with a pre-loaded spoon and took her time exploring finger foods before putting them to her mouth. She would carefully chew and hardly gagged compared to my firstborn. After a couple of months, her preference moved towards finger foods, but she would still accept a spoon sometimes which worked for us. This just highlights how you can do similar things as a parent/caregiver and yet babies will respond differently based on their personality. If you aren't specifically drawn to one method, you can offer both and be led by your baby, particularly if you prefer the flexibility.

THE PRINCIPLES OF WEANING

Milk

From six months onwards, cow's milk or fortified alternative milks such as soy, pea or oat milk can be used in cooking or mixed with porridge/cereals. The main milk drink should always be breast milk or infant formula until your baby is around 12 months. Unless specified by a health practitioner (for example, for allergy reasons), most babies will be receiving enough nutrients from solid foods and will not need formula over the age of one. Full-fat or semi-skimmed cow's milk or fortified alternative milks can be given as a drink from 12 months (more on this on page 43) and 'growing up' or toddler milks are unnecessary.

There are still many benefits to continuing breastfeeding past 12 months if it works for you and your little one. You might be setting goals such as 'I need to stop breastfeeding by X month in time for work', but returning to work really does not have to be the end of your breastfeeding journey if you don't want it to be. You should notify your employer if you wish to continue so they can carry out a risk assessment and make sure they are offering you an appropriate space to pump milk and store it safely in the fridge. I returned to work after my first baby at 13 months and unexpectedly continued to breastfeed until 25 months as I just didn't feel ready to stop. I chose not to pump (unless I felt engorged) as my eldest still wasn't reliably drinking milk from a cup after turning one and my milk supply seemed to adapt during my days at work. Babies are great at catching up before/after work and I continued to breastfeed on demand on our days off together (and overnight until 16 months). My point is to do what works for you and your family – please don't feel pressured by anyone to go against yours or your baby's needs, especially due to logistics.

Building a Balanced Meal

Now you've chosen which weaning method seems best suited for your family, let's look at how you can ensure you are meeting your baby's nutritional needs without spending hours in the kitchen.

It's our responsibility as caregivers to offer our child a plate with a balance of foods and it's our child's job to decide what they want to eat during that meal. So, how do you ensure you are giving your little one the best opportunity to obtain all of the nutrients they need? Firstly, it's helpful to understand what nutrients they need. These can be divided into macronutrients, which are where the bulk of their energy comes from, and vitamins and minerals, also known as micronutrients, which are only needed in small amounts but are vital for their development.

I don't want to bore you with the science, but I do think it helps to know what nutrients we need at each meal to make sure you are providing opportunities for your baby to absorb all the vitamins and minerals they need. On the next page we'll go through each of the most common and essential nutrients with example foods to make it easy. You may already think of building meals in this way, but if you don't, this is a great time to start thinking about how to create healthier habits for the whole family.

Why nutrition matters

There is a growing body of research to suggest that the first 1,000 days of your child's life can have lifelong consequences on their health and well-being. This critical period starts from conception and continues while they are in the womb until your child is around two years of age. During this time, the foundations are laid down for their physical, social, emotional and cognitive (brain) development. Your little one's brain has a wonderful ability to adapt to its physical and social surroundings in a concept called 'plasticity', which is highest in the first 1,000 days and is what makes their environment so important at this stage.

The three fundamental pillars to the first 1,000 days are:

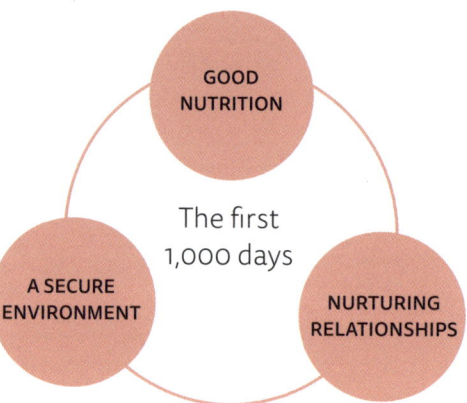

During these transformative early years, the human brain has the highest nutrient requirements because it is undergoing a period of rapid growth. These nutrients include macronutrients such as protein, carbohydrates and fats, as well as micronutrients such as iron, zinc, iodine, B vitamins and vitamin A and K (we'll look at these in detail and what each is used for below). Playing a consistent and active role in meeting these demands can help your baby to thrive, grow and learn. Nutrition also plays a key role in your baby's developing immune, hormonal, musculoskeletal, metabolic and gastrointestinal system.

The 'first 1,000 days' concept has now become a part of many government-led initiatives worldwide and I truly believe that every parent/caregiver should be given the opportunity and support to give their child the best start in life to help them to reach their potential. It is also reassuring to know that if you had a tough pregnancy and were unable to eat the nutritious foods you would have liked to, it is not too late to be able to make a difference as babies' brains are so versatile at this age.

Macronutrients

Macronutrients are the nutrients your baby needs in larger amounts to provide energy for healthy growth and development. They are broadly classified into three categories: carbohydrates, proteins and fats, and are all equally important in the diet.

Carbohydrates

Carbohydrates are the body's main source of energy. Once eaten, they are broken down into glucose which provides fuel to your baby's muscles and brain. Some starchy carbohydrate examples include bread, pasta, rice and potato. Fruit and vegetables are also carbohydrates and provide a good source of vitamins and minerals, so are encouraged on your baby's plate from the get-go. The more colours and different types of fruit and vegetables you can expose your baby to, the wider the variety of different vitamins and minerals you are offering them. This includes chopped, frozen or tinned options which may be cheaper and more convenient, and can still be as nutritious, if not more so, than fresh fruit and vegetables.

Wholegrain carbohydrates, such as brown rice, wholemeal bread or wholewheat pasta, tend to be high in fibre, which helps to promote a healthy digestive system and 'good' bacteria in the gut. However, it is generally recommended not to *only* give wholegrain foods to your baby as the high fibre can quickly fill up their tummy before they have had a chance to eat all the nutrients and energy they need. It is best to give a mixture of wholegrain and white starchy carbohydrates at the start of weaning. After your baby turns two, you can gradually introduce more wholegrain foods.

Protein

Protein is essential for growth and repair and helps to produce hormones, support the immune system, strengthen the skin and move other nutrients around the body. Protein is found in animal products such as meat, fish and eggs, as well as plant-based products such as beans, lentils and tofu. You might be worried that if your little one hasn't taken well to the texture of meat they are not meeting their protein requirements, but protein can still be found in carbohydrate-rich and fatty foods. For example, dairy foods such as yoghurt and cheese contain lots of protein too and adding nut butters to meals can also boost protein. Choosing iron-rich sources of protein are ideal at mealtimes to maximise iron absorption (see page 32).

Fats and oils

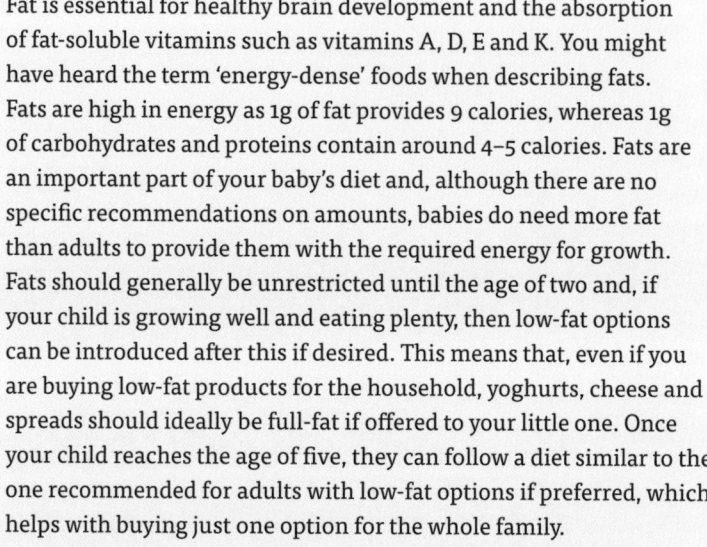

Fat is essential for healthy brain development and the absorption of fat-soluble vitamins such as vitamins A, D, E and K. You might have heard the term 'energy-dense' foods when describing fats. Fats are high in energy as 1g of fat provides 9 calories, whereas 1g of carbohydrates and proteins contain around 4–5 calories. Fats are an important part of your baby's diet and, although there are no specific recommendations on amounts, babies do need more fat than adults to provide them with the required energy for growth. Fats should generally be unrestricted until the age of two and, if your child is growing well and eating plenty, then low-fat options can be introduced after this if desired. This means that, even if you are buying low-fat products for the household, yoghurts, cheese and spreads should ideally be full-fat if offered to your little one. Once your child reaches the age of five, they can follow a diet similar to the one recommended for adults with low-fat options if preferred, which helps with buying just one option for the whole family.

While different types of fat can impact our health in different ways – for example, saturated fat commonly found in cakes or biscuits should be consumed in moderation as it can increase our risk of high cholesterol and heart disease – we don't need to 'fear' giving our babies fats. Aim to provide fats from animal products such as lean meat, fish, dairy or eggs, or plant-based products such as olive oil, ground nuts or avocados. Omega-3 fatty acids such as DHA and EHA found in oily fish, nuts and seeds are particularly important for early brain development and function.

It can feel all-consuming thinking 'what should I make for my baby's next meal?', but as long as you are offering something from each of the categories above, you will help your baby to meet their nutritional needs. If you don't have time to cook a meal or don't want to buy lots of ingredients, you can whip up something you may already have at home, such as bread (carbohydrate), egg (iron-rich protein), cheese (fat/dairy) and cucumber (fruit/veg) – it does not have to be a conventional meal or anything fancy. I find that if you have a strategy for how to put a meal together, all the rest easily falls into place. Don't worry though – you will find lots of examples of balanced meals and recipe ideas in Part Two (pages 118–247) so you don't have to think of them all by yourself!

It's worth remembering that variety is key to ensure your baby is being exposed to a broad range of flavours and textures. The more variety you are able to offer, not only does it mean your baby will be getting a broad range of nutrients, but it *may* also help to create more adventurous eaters and reduce the likelihood or severity of fussy eating. You may find that it takes your baby 10–15 exposures (or more) to a new food before they accept or consume it, so try not to take foods that they are not interested in off the menu and continue to give them the opportunity to explore it. I know it's frustrating if they are only picking it up, mushing it into the highchair or throwing it on the floor, but these are all small steps in the process of learning to eat new foods.

Vitamins and minerals

Vitamins and minerals – micronutrients – are important to keep us healthy and help our bodies to function. They support healthy growth and development in children by helping their cells and organs carry out the jobs they need to do, such as regulating hormones, helping their immune systems fight infection and support wound healing. We aren't able to make vitamins and minerals naturally, so we obtain them from the food we eat, with the exception of vitamin D where the main source is sunlight in summer months. Vitamins and minerals are only needed in small amounts compared to macronutrients and, although they don't directly give us energy, they are needed for our bodies to obtain the energy from macronutrients.

In this section, we will briefly look at the important micronutrients babies need to thrive, their role in the body and what foods they can be found in. This is not an exhaustive list, but given there are 13 essential vitamins and hundreds of minerals, it would be overwhelming to mention them all. I also would not recommend trying to monitor daily amounts of individual vitamins and minerals in your baby's food as this is unrealistic. Just be aware of offering them a variety of healthy foods when you are putting a plate together and making choices about which foods to offer – your little one should then be able to easily obtain exactly what they need.

Iron

Babies need more iron from the age of six to twelve months than at any other time in their childhood. It is one of the most critical nutrients for brain development. According to the WHO, iron deficiency is the most common nutritional deficiency that we see globally, particularly in children. Iron is needed for red blood cells to carry oxygen around the body and support your child's ability to grow and learn. Most babies are born with enough iron stores to last approximately six months (this may be less if you were iron-deficient in pregnancy or your baby was born very small). One of the reasons babies are encouraged to start weaning from approximately six months of age is to obtain enough iron to keep up with their growing demands.

Breast milk contains small amounts of iron, but it is more easily absorbed by the body. Infant formula contains large amounts of supplemented iron, but it is not as easily absorbed by the body. Try to serve your baby an iron-rich food with as many meals as you can when starting solids.

THE PRINCIPLES OF WEANING

Animal sources of iron include **red meat**, **chicken**, **eggs** and **fish**. Plant-based sources include **fortified cereals**, **dark-green leafy vegetables**, **pulses** (beans, peas and lentils), **nut butters** and **tofu**, though plant-based sources of iron are less easily absorbed by the body. Vitamin C can help the body absorb more iron from food, so pairing iron-rich foods with vitamin C-rich foods, such as citrus fruits, berries, tomatoes and sweet potatoes, can help to increase your baby's iron uptake. If you are following a purely vegetarian or vegan diet, it is worth speaking to your family doctor or a paediatric dietitian to make sure your baby's nutritional needs are being met. (See page 42 for more on vegan/vegetarian diets.)

Symptoms of iron deficiency anaemia

Some children with mild iron deficiency anaemia may not show any symptoms at all, but, if they do, the common ones include:

- pale skin
- lack of energy
- tiredness
- breathlessness
- loss of appetite
- developmental delays

The symptoms can be vague, making it difficult for parents/caregivers to recognise them, so it is always worth having a chat to your family doctor or paediatrician if you have any concerns. They will ask some more detailed questions in the first instance and may offer a blood test to check iron levels if necessary. Doctors will seek to correct iron levels with a liquid supplement if they are found to be low.

Vitamin C

Vitamin C is important for your child's general health and immune system. As discussed, it helps the body absorb more iron when served with iron-rich foods. Other functions include maintaining healthy skin, blood vessels, bones and cartilage. Vitamin C also plays a role in helping with tissue repair and wound healing.

We always seem to associate citrus fruits such as oranges and lemons with high levels of vitamin C, but other fruits and vegetables can be great sources too, including herbs such as parsley. Vegetables containing high levels of vitamin C include **bell peppers**, **broccoli** and **Brussels sprouts**, while vitamin C-rich fruits include **strawberries**, **kiwis**, **tomatoes** and **blackcurrants**.

Lack of vitamin C can lead to a rare condition called scurvy which includes symptoms of tiredness, irritability, joint/muscle pain, bleeding gums or skin that bruises easily. Although it is rare in the UK, babies and children can be at higher risk particularly if there are no fresh fruit or vegetables included in their diet for long periods of time. It is important to treat scurvy quickly, however, most people will go on to make a full recovery.

Vitamin D

Vitamin D is an essential vitamin to keep bones, teeth and muscles healthy by regulating calcium and phosphate in the body. Lack of vitamin D can lead to bone disorders such as rickets (softening of bones) in children. Although, overall, rates of rickets are low in the UK, there has been a rise over recent years.

The main source of vitamin D is **sunlight**, but dietary sources include **egg yolk**, **oily fish**, **red meat** and fortified products such as **cereals**, **milk**, **yoghurt** and **tofu**. It is difficult to get enough vitamin D from food alone, therefore current guidance recommends a vitamin D supplement all year round specifically for:

- ✓ babies (drinking less than 500ml infant formula/day)
- ✓ children aged one to four years
- ✓ pregnant or breastfeeding women
- ✓ all adults and children in autumn/winter

> Breastfed babies are recommended to have a vitamin D supplement of 8.5–10mcg per day from birth regardless of the mother's vitamin D intake to ensure they are obtaining enough.

B Vitamins

Children who have a balanced and varied diet along with meat and dairy are likely to have sufficient levels of B vitamins. There are eight different types of B vitamins which play specific roles in our bodies, including maintaining a healthy nervous system, eye and skin health, and helping to release energy from food. Some of the most important and well-known vitamins are vitamin B9 (folate) and vitamin B12, which are essential to forming red blood cells which carry oxygen around the body. I have included a table below listing all eight B vitamins with good food sources and the individual roles they play within our bodies.

B VITAMIN	ROLE	GOOD FOOD SOURCES
B1: Thiamin	Helps the body break down and release energy from food. Maintains a healthy nervous system.	• peas • some fresh fruits (such as bananas and oranges) • nuts • wholegrain breads • some fortified breakfast cereals • liver (avoid if you are pregnant)
B2: Riboflavin	Keeps skin, eyes and the nervous system healthy. Helps the body release energy from food.	• milk • eggs • fortified breakfast cereals • mushrooms • plain yoghurt (Keep these foods out of sunlight which can destroy riboflavin)
B3: Niacin	• Helps the body release energy from food. • Keeps the nervous system and skin healthy.	• meat • fish • wheat flour • eggs
B5: Pantothenic acid	Several functions including helping the body release energy from food.	• most vegetables, wholegrain foods and meat • chicken • beef • liver and kidneys (avoid liver if you are pregnant) • eggs • mushrooms • avocado • some fortified breakfast cereals

B VITAMIN	ROLE	GOOD FOOD SOURCES
B6: **Pyridoxine**	• Helps the body to use and store energy from protein and carbohydrates in food. • Helps the body to make haemoglobin in red blood cells that transports oxygen around the body.	• pork • poultry, such as chicken or turkey • some fish • peanuts • soy beans • wheatgerm • oats • bananas • milk • some fortified breakfast cereals
B7: **Biotin**	• Needed in very small amounts to help the body make fatty acids. • Naturally occurring bacteria in the gut make biotin so unclear if needed in the diet.	Found in small amounts in lots of foods, such as: • meats • egg • fish • legumes • nuts and seeds • bananas • milk
B9: **Folate, also known as folic acid**	• Helps the body make healthy red blood cells. • Helps to reduce the risk of birth defects called neural tube defects, such as spina bifida in unborn babies.	• broccoli • Brussels sprouts • leafy green vegetables, such as cabbage, kale, spring greens and spinach • peas • chickpeas and kidney beans • liver (avoid if you are pregnant) • fortified breakfast cereals
B12: **Cyanocobalamin**	• Helps to make red blood cells and keep the nervous system healthy. • Helps to release energy from food. • Helps the body to use folate.	• meat • fish • milk • cheese • eggs • some fortified breakfast cereals

Vitamin A

Vitamin A supports the immune system against illness and infection. It also helps with vision in dim light, maintaining skin health and supporting the lining of some parts of the body such as the nose. As the body can store vitamin A that it does not need right away, you don't need to eat it every day.

Good sources of vitamin A include **cheese, eggs, oily fish, milk** and **yoghurt. Liver products** such as pâté are particularly rich in vitamin A so babies and children should not eat them more than once a week (and pregnant women should not eat them at all as too much can harm an unborn baby).

You can also include sources of beta-carotene in your baby's diet as it is converted to vitamin A by the body. Good sources of beta-carotene are yellow and orange fruit and vegetables such as **mango, papaya, carrots, sweet potatoes** and **bell peppers** and **leafy greens** such as spinach.

Zinc

Zinc is an important mineral for making new cells, healing wounds, supporting babies' immune systems and helping the body to process macronutrients. Like iron, breast milk can support zinc needs until babies are around six months, before levels decline and they start to rely more on solids for their intake. Infant formula contains zinc, however, it is less bioavailable (less easily absorbed by the body) than in breast milk. Zinc is not stored by the body so it's important to try to include it in your baby's diet daily.

Good sources of zinc include **meat, shellfish, dairy, bread** and **cereals**. If your baby is following a vegan or vegetarian diet, zinc is less easily absorbed from plant-based foods as they contain substances such as phytates which can reduce the absorption of zinc.

Iodine

Iodine is a mineral that helps to make thyroid hormones which control metabolism and support healthy growth and development. The main sources of iodine include **cow's milk, dairy products, white fish** and **eggs**. Iodine can be found in plant-based foods such as **cereals** and **grains**, but the amount may vary depending on the levels found in the soil that the plants are grown in. Vegetarians who are consuming dairy products or pescatarians will still be obtaining iodine. If you are following a vegan diet, see the advice on page 42.

Calcium

Calcium is essential in building bones, preserving dental health and regulating muscle contractions as well as the clotting of blood. Low calcium can lead to rickets in children and osteomalacia (softening of the bones) or osteoporosis (thinning of the bones) in later life. Sources of calcium include:

- **dairy:** milk, cheese, yoghurt
- **fruit/vegetables:** green vegetables such as broccoli or kale, and fruit such as oranges or kiwis
- **fortified dairy alternatives:** oat milk, soy milk, soy yoghurt, pea milk, calcium-set tofu
- **fish with crushed bones** such as tinned salmon/sardines
- **fortified foods** such as breads and cereals (for example, Ready Brek)

Below are the UK daily calcium recommendations (note guidelines in other countries significantly differ):

- **Under 1 year:** 525mg (largely obtained from milk)
- **1–3 years:** 350mg
- **Adults:** 700mg
- **Breastfeeding adults:** 1,250mg

You are not expected to calculate exactly how much calcium your child is consuming daily, but it's good to have a rough idea of amounts as having lots of dairy can cause some children to become constipated. Approximate examples of 50mg of calcium include (brands will vary):

- 7.5g cheddar cheese
- 40ml cow's/ fortified soy milk
- 30g yoghurt/ fortified soy yoghurt
- 30g calcium-set tofu
- 12.5g sardines
- 1 large orange
- 110g broccoli
- ½ heaped teaspoon tahini
- 1 thin slice white bread

To meet an average one-year-old's daily calcium requirements, all they need to consume is 160ml of cow's (or soy) milk, which could be in their cereal, 1 slice of white bread, 7.5g of cheese and 30g of yoghurt. This is not including any breast milk or infant formula they may still be consuming, which would also contribute to calcium intake, meaning they would need less from solid food. This is why I often tell parents/caregivers not to worry if their one-year-old is not drinking much milk at nursery from a cup as there are plenty of other ways to obtain calcium in their diet. I hope it also provides some reassurance that there are plenty of non-dairy sources of calcium if your little one has cow's milk protein allergy (see page 61) or has significantly reduced their milk intake after one year.

If you are providing your child with dairy alternatives such as oat, soy, pea or coconut milk, it is worth checking they have been fortified with calcium before offering them to your baby. (See the box on page 43 for more on alternative milks.)

Plant-based, vegetarian and vegan diets

Some families may choose for their children to follow a more plant-based, vegetarian or vegan diet. There are lots of benefits to consuming a more plant-based diet, with many studies in adults showing a reduced risk of developing long-term diseases such as heart disease, high blood pressure and obesity. Research so far has shown a plant-based diet will not cause any major health disadvantages if it is carefully planned.

It's worth noting that there are no recommended vegan formulas in the UK (soy-based formula is not currently recommended before six months). One of the ways your child can stay vegan prior to starting solids is through exclusive breastfeeding, but, of course, that may not be an option for everyone for a variety of reasons.

There are some additional things to consider for babies who follow a vegan diet to make sure they are still getting all the nutrients they need. Vitamin B12 and iodine are predominantly found in meat, fish and dairy products, which means those who are following a vegan diet would need to rely on fortified food sources and/or supplements to obtain these nutrients. Minerals such as iron and zinc are less bioavailable in plant-based foods. While some omega-3 fatty acids (ALA) can be found in plant-based foods, such as nuts and leafy vegetables, omega-3s such as EPA and DHA can only be found in fish. This means it will be more challenging to meet these requirements from a vegan diet and supplementation may be needed. Vegans will also need to pay closer attention to sources of protein and fats in the diet. I highly recommend speaking to a specialist dietitian who can closely assess the foods in your baby's diet and decide if/when supplementation may be needed.

Vitamin supplements

The UK government currently recommends all babies are given a vitamin supplement of A, C and D from 6 months' to 5 years' old, unless they drink more than 500mls of infant formula per day as it is already fortified with vitamins.

Some vitamin supplements contain other vitamins and minerals so it is worth having a chat with your pharmacist about which supplement may be suitable for your child. It is always advised to follow the recommended dose on the label as consuming too much of some vitamins can be harmful.

Alternative milks

Nutritionally, cow's milk is still the milk of choice for growing children when looking specifically at energy, protein, calcium, iodine and B vitamins. However, your child may have a dairy allergy or you may decide this is not the best option for your family, especially if you are following a plant-based diet.

Below I have compiled a list of things to think about when choosing an alternative milk for your baby:

FORTIFICATION
Milks which contain added essential nutrients such as calcium, iodine, vitamins B12 and B2, and vitamin D are beneficial. Organic milks aren't fortified so are generally not recommended.

CALORIES
Full fat cow's milk contains 60–65 calories/100ml, so picking a close alternative (ideally more than 40–45 calories/100ml) can help to meet your baby's energy requirements.

PROTEIN
Dairy is an important source of protein for children. Therefore, opting for milks with higher protein such as soy and pea is ideal unless there are allergies.

ADDED SUGARS
Some milks are sweetened with added sugars which can contribute to tooth decay. Opting for unsweetened versions is ideal unless advised otherwise.

NUT MILKS
These are not usually recommended as they do not contain enough calories or protein for little ones. Rice milks should also be avoided under the age of five years as they may contain too much arsenic (see page 51).

The cost of fortified milk alternatives varies widely so it's worth shopping around to see what fits within your budget if you will be buying them regularly. Don't forget to shake fortified milk alternatives before drinking them as some of the added nutrients can remain in the sediment at the bottom.

Things to Watch Out For

While weaning can be a fun and enjoyable experience, there are some instances which can take you by surprise if you are not expecting them, such as gagging. I want to mention them here so you know what to expect and can stay calm during those moments when you may feel out of control. It's also important to spot when there may be something serious happening, such as choking. Parents/caregivers understandably worry so much about choking, whether they are spoon-feeding or baby-led weaning, so, although it is a rare occurrence, I think it's important to highlight how to prevent it, how to recognise it and how to manage it. I have also listed foods to avoid which may pose a risk to your baby and alternatives you can offer.

Gagging versus choking

Gagging is very common when babies are starting solids and is a completely normal response to protect their airway from becoming blocked. The gag reflex is highly sensitive while babies are learning to move food around their mouth and chew. It can sound and look alarming, but try not to intervene as it may make things worse and lead to choking. Let your little one figure it out and try to stay calm for a positive eating experience for all (easier said than done, I know!). Parents/caregivers who feel particularly anxious may find it helpful to join in with mealtimes and eat some finger food themselves, to take the pressure off from both sides.

    Choking, on the other hand, is rare and an absolute medical emergency. It is important to always supervise your baby while they are eating as choking can be silent so you may not hear if you need to intervene. If you notice your child turning pale/blue* or they stop breathing/making any noise, you must begin first aid by immediately removing them from the highchair and performing back blows with the heel of your hand.

---

*Note: babies of darker skin colour may not obviously change skin colour, but the inside of their lips/nails may start to turn blue.

Gagging versus choking

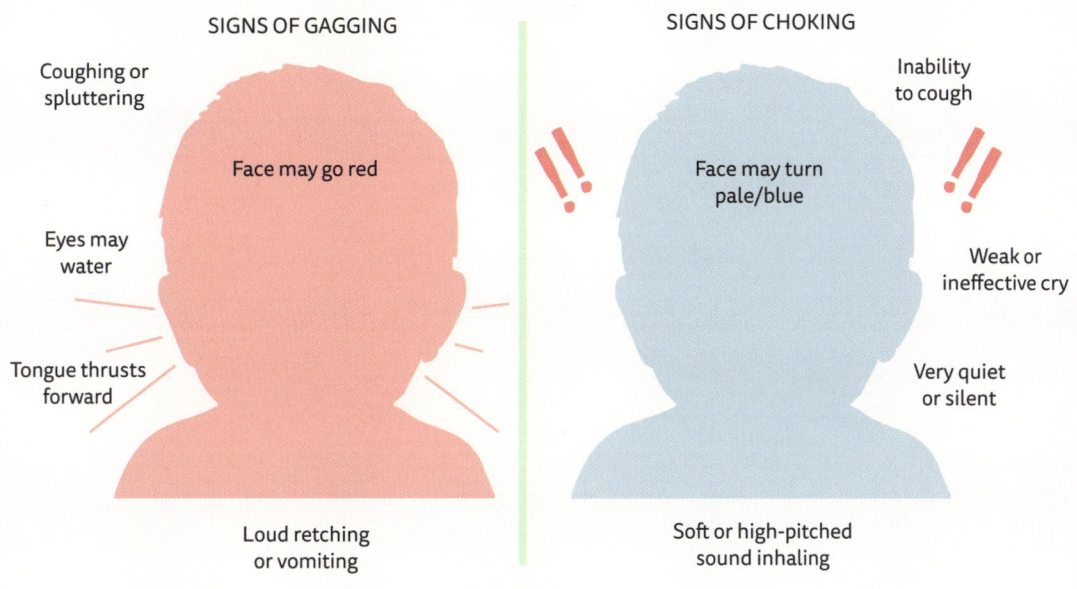

SIGNS OF GAGGING
- Coughing or spluttering
- Face may go red
- Eyes may water
- Tongue thrusts forward
- Loud retching or vomiting

SIGNS OF CHOKING
- Inability to cough
- Face may turn pale/blue
- Weak or ineffective cry
- Very quiet or silent
- Soft or high-pitched sound inhaling

How to reduce the risk of choking

Seating: always ensure your child is seated in the correct position at a 90-degree angle (avoid feeding solids in reclined car seats, prams or bouncers where possible, especially at the start of weaning when your baby is learning how to chew and swallow).

Finger foods: appropriately steam or cook finger foods to ensure they are soft enough to mush between your finger and thumb with a gentle push. Slice into narrow batons or cut round foods in half. Remove any hard skins, pits, stones and bones (see page 47 for more on adapting foods for babies).

Environment: ensure it is distraction-free and calm, and that there is plenty of time for your baby to eat.

Role model: show your little one how to take small bites, chew and then swallow.

Supervise: carefully observe your baby eating at all times and be ready to jump in should a rare emergency such as choking arise.

Choking hazards: avoid until your child is developmentally ready (see page 46).

Common choking hazards

Children under the age of five are at highest risk of choking while eating as they are still learning how to chew and swallow food properly. They may swallow food whole, which can block their narrow airway leading to choking. Any food can present as a choking hazard, however there are some which carry a higher risk unless they have been adapted accordingly (such as cutting grapes into quarters or squishing blueberries). Generally speaking, high-risk foods tend to be firm, sticky, chewy, crunchy, round and/or even slippery.

Common culprits include:

FRUIT AND VEGETABLES:
- uncut grapes, cherry tomatoes, berries
- unsquashed peas, sweetcorn
- hard raw fruits and vegetables (such as apple or carrot batons)
- dried fruit or vegetables (such as raisins)
- hard pips and stones in fruit (always remove)

PROTEINS:
- whole nuts or seeds
- large spoonfuls of nut/seed butters on their own
- tough pieces of meat
- hot dogs and other sausages (unsliced)
- whole beans (and chickpeas)
- solid blocks of cheese
- skin, fat and bones in meat or fish (always remove)

GRAIN PRODUCTS:
- popcorn, pretzels, crisps or equivalent
- crackers or teething biscuits
- white or seeded breads
- granola bars/chewy fruit snacks

SWEETS:
- round or hard candy, jelly beans, gummy snacks
- marshmallows
- raw jelly cubes

Although the foods opposite are 'high risk', there may be some babies who quickly learn to handle some of them by biting and chewing carefully, whereas others may struggle even after the age of one. This is why it is so important to look at your baby as an individual and monitor how their feeding skills progress. I was far more confident giving my youngest a breadstick at ten months as she was meticulously biting and chewing, whereas I held off on my eldest until just after he turned one.

I would strongly advise altering all of these foods to begin with to make them safer (see table below). I personally avoided giving dried fruit, whole nuts (see below), popcorn, pretzels, teething biscuits or any type of sweets to my children until they were at least over two years old. I would adapt to your little one's feeding skills and, if in any doubt, it is best to wait until the risk decreases after the age of four.

Common choking hazard	How to adapt
BREAD	Toast before offering to baby
BLOCKS OF CHEESE	Offer to baby grated
CHERRY TOMATOES, GRAPES, BERRIES	Cut into quarters
HARD, RAW VEGETABLES	Cut into batons and steam until soft enough to squash between finger and thumb
PEAS, SWEETCORN, BEANS	Squash flat before serving
NUT BUTTERS	Dilute with water or add to baking/porridge
CHUNKS OF MEAT	Cook until tender and finely shred
HARD FRUITS SUCH AS APPLES/PEARS	Steam, poach or even grate ripe fruit
HOT DOGS AND SAUSAGES	Slice lengthways and remove skin
WHOLE NUTS	Chop, grind or flake nuts into foods, such as porridge

Foods to avoid

What you choose to feed your baby is a personal choice. However, there are some foods that are advised against for health and safety reasons.

Honey

Honey may occasionally contain a toxin (clostridium botulinum spores) leading to a rare but life-threatening illness for babies. It is best to avoid until your baby is at least 12 months old. You can try date syrup instead to sweeten recipes, although you may want to delay very sweet-tasting foods until your child is closer to two years old to reduce the risk of them developing a preference for sweet foods.

Added salt

Babies' kidneys are still maturing, so they may not be able to process too much salt. There is some research to suggest that excessive salt in childhood could potentially increase the risk of high blood pressure in later life, although much more research is needed. Try to avoid adding extra salt when cooking unless you are batch cooking in large quantities for the whole family and use zero- or low-salt stock cubes. Aim for less than 1g salt per day until your baby is 12 months old, which is about 3 slices of white bread, 60g of cheddar cheese or 10 tall breadsticks. If your baby does have a meal that contains more salt, don't worry – just keep an eye on their meals for the rest of the day or week. There are lots of ways to add flavour to food without using salt, such as using different herbs and spices, which you will find in the recipes in Part Two (see page 118).

Specific salty foods to avoid include crisps, ready meals, takeaways, sausages, bacon, chips with salt, cured meats and condiments.

Added sugar

There is no specific guidance on how much sugar babies should be having under the age of four. However, we know that sugar contributes to tooth decay so it is best to try to avoid offering refined sugary foods (such as chocolate, sweets and biscuits) regularly until your baby is closer to two years old, when they have more awareness of the sweet foods available. Filling up their little tummies with sugar may also displace room for other nutrient-rich foods. Naturally occurring sugars such as fruit are perfectly fine and best offered as part of or straight after a meal to help protect your baby's teeth.

How to look after baby's teeth

Looking after milk teeth helps to cement good lifelong habits. You can start brushing your baby's teeth with a baby toothbrush as soon as they come through twice a day with a smear of fluoride toothpaste. It is easiest to sit your baby on your lap with their head leaning against your chest. Brush their teeth in small circular motions until you have reached all tooth surfaces. Don't worry if you don't manage to brush much on each occasion – it's more about building a habit that becomes part of your child's routine. Setting a good example by showing babies how we look after our own teeth is the best way for them to learn.

Avoid giving your child any fluids overnight that are not breast milk, infant formula or water to help protect their teeth. Take your baby to your own dental appointments so they become familiar with the idea. The current recommendation is for children to see a dentist when their first milk teeth appear and typically six-monthly thereafter unless told otherwise.

The 2024 national oral health survey showed approximately one in five children had obvious tooth decay by the age of five. The amount and frequency of free sugars consumed is the main causative factor, hence, tooth decay is largely preventable. The main symptoms include pain, infection, difficulty eating, speaking and sleeping. The early loss of baby teeth due to tooth decay can lead to crowding and incorrect positioning of the emerging adult tooth. Tooth decay in baby teeth can also lead to infection of the underlying adult tooth with potential damage or even loss of the adult tooth.

Whole nuts and peanuts

Whole nuts and peanuts should be avoided in children under five years old to minimise the risk of choking. You can offer ground nuts or smooth nut butters from six months (or earlier if you have been advised to by a doctor due to a high risk of allergies), though remember not to serve nut/seed butters on their own as they can be a choking hazard unless thinned down sufficiently with water. You can sprinkle ground nuts or drizzle nut butters into porridge or baked goods or even stir them into meals.

Unpasteurised cheese

Babies can eat pasteurised full-fat cheese from six months old, including hard cheese, cottage cheese or cream cheese. Some cheese varieties are high in salt so you may want to opt for lower salt options such as Emmental or mozzarella, or you can rinse cottage cheese in water to reduce the sodium levels.

Babies should avoid the following cheeses until they are at least 12 months old due to the risk of them containing the bacteria listeria:

- mould-ripened soft cheeses such as Brie or Camembert
- mould-ripened goat's milk soft cheese like chèvre
- soft blue-veined cheese like Roquefort
- cheese made from unpasteurised milk (always check the label)

The risk tends to reduce as your baby gets older. The above cheeses can be used as part of a cooked recipe – for example, baked Camembert – as listeria is killed by cooking.

Raw egg

This is due to the risk of salmonella infection and includes partially cooked eggs too. It is best to avoid giving your baby home-made mayonnaise, raw cake mixtures or home-made desserts with uncooked hens' eggs. In the UK, if eggs are marked with the red British Lion stamp or say 'British Lion Quality' with a red lion on the box, then there is a much lower risk of salmonella and they can be partially cooked, for example, in the form of soft-boiled eggs. If the eggs are unmarked then it is best to cook them until the egg yolk and white are both solid. The same applies to duck, goose or quail eggs.

Raw shellfish

Raw or lightly cooked shellfish such as mussels, oysters or clams can increase the risk of food poisoning so are best to avoid serving to babies unless fully cooked.

Swordfish, marlin and shark

These contain high levels of mercury which can affect the development of a baby's nervous system so should be avoided altogether.

Rice milk

Children under five years old should not have rice drinks as a substitute for breast milk, infant formula or cow's milk as they may contain too much arsenic. Arsenic is a metal element that is found naturally in the environment such as in soil and rocks. It can then find its way into our food and water.

Rice tends to absorb more arsenic than other grains, but this does not mean that you or your baby cannot eat rice. In the UK, there are maximum levels of inorganic arsenic allowed in rice and rice products, and even stricter levels are set for foods intended for young children. Rinsing basmati rice with water has shown to decrease the level of arsenic by 10 per cent, and even further if the rice is cooked in a high volume of water. The only downside is that rinsing also removes nutrients such as iron and folate in the process.

Don't worry if your child has already had rice drinks. There's no immediate risk to them, but it is best to switch to a different kind of milk as they may contain too much arsenic.

Slushies

Slushies often contain an ingredient called glycerol which can cause young children to experience headaches or nausea. Although it is unlikely to be harmful at low levels, too much glycerol can lead to low blood sugar, dizziness and confusion. The effects are thought to be related to body weight. The Food Standards Agency currently advises slushies should be avoided until children are at least over the age of four years old, and children under ten years old should avoid refills.

Navigating Allergies

It can feel like there is a lot to navigate with weaning already, then allergies are thrown into the mix and it's no wonder you can find yourself in a bit of a head spin. If allergies are already on your radar, then this is good news as allergy awareness is increasing, especially with up to 4-5 per cent of babies in the UK affected.

With the changes in advice over the last decade, such as encouraging parents/caregivers to introduce allergens sooner rather than later and the worry it causes so many of us, I really wanted to include a comprehensive yet easy to understand section on navigating allergies, so you have all the relevant information at your fingertips. I also think it is important to talk about how to spot a reaction and what you should do to keep your baby as safe as possible to take away some of that uncertainty. The link with the skin condition eczema is also confusing, so I have delved into what the science shows and how to manage this too. In the next chapter, we'll look at how to introduce allergens safely when weaning your baby (see page 84).

What causes allergies?

Experts are still trying to understand the process that leads to someone developing an allergy. Interestingly, certain allergies are more common depending on how much they are eaten in a particular country – for example, nut allergy is more common in the UK and US, whereas chickpea allergy is more common in India. Many people assume that babies are born with food allergies, but we now know they develop after birth due to a combination of genetic and environmental factors. It is believed that a complex reaction between a food allergen in the environment and the immune system occurs through the skin which causes an allergy. This is why it's so important not to rub allergens on the skin before weaning, which was sometimes advised many years ago.

You can follow all the guidance below on preventing food allergies and your baby may still develop a food allergy, so please do remember that **allergies are nobody's fault**, and it may simply be related to your baby having a strong genetic tendency.

What does the research say?

Advice has now changed about how to introduce allergens to babies following two major studies (LEAP and EAT). The research found that, in high-risk babies, early introduction of allergens such as egg and peanuts from four months significantly reduced the risk of a child developing that food allergy. Children were continuously given the allergen three times a week. If children did not continue to keep the allergen in their diet after it had been introduced, this benefit of a reduced allergy risk was not seen (I've included advice in the next chapter on maintaining food allergens in your baby's diet for this reason – see page 87).

Interestingly, a recent follow-up study has shown that children who had consumed regular, frequent peanut until the age of five still had a reduced risk of developing a peanut allergy in adolescence regardless of how much peanut was consumed after the age of five. Follow-up studies are still ongoing, but this could suggest potential lifelong protection against developing allergies through early and regular exposure as a baby and toddler. It is important to note that the strongest benefit was seen in 'high-risk' babies, but most allergies develop in children who are low risk. However, we do know that delaying allergen introduction after 12 months may actually increase the risk of *any* child developing an allergy to that food.

Who is high risk?

Your baby is defined as 'high risk' if they have a known food allergy and/or moderate to severe eczema. The risk is higher if eczema started before three months of age and if it is poorly controlled or inflamed at the time of allergen introduction. Although children do not inherit a food allergy from their parent with a food allergy, they may develop a genetic susceptibility and a tendency to eczema, which is a key risk factor. A sibling having a food allergy does not automatically increase the risk of your baby developing a food allergy (unless you delay allergy introduction due to the sibling having an allergy, but understandably this can be a difficult decision). If someone in your home suffers with a food allergy, careful planning is needed if deciding to introduce the allergen to your baby in order to keep the allergic person safe. You can speak to your family doctor or an allergy specialist for further advice if you are worried. It's worth noting that, generally, serious reactions only occur after eating the allergen rather than simply being exposed to it.

Baby eczema

Atopic eczema is the most common form of eczema in children and often develops before their first birthday. It can run in families and tends to develop alongside conditions such as asthma and hay fever, which typically come later. Eczema can cause the skin to become itchy, dry, cracked and sore. Some babies will have small patches, while, for others, it may be all over their body. Triggers include soaps, detergents, the weather, stress and food allergies but the underlying cause is genetic. There is no cure for eczema although it typically improves over time. The symptoms can be controlled by using moisturising creams daily to protect the skin barrier. Your doctor may also prescribe topical steroid cream to reduce redness and itching during a flare.

Babies with eczema have a slightly higher risk of developing food allergies. However, there are lots of babies with eczema who do not go on to develop food allergies. Current research suggests that, while certain foods can trigger eczema 'flare-ups', food allergy does not commonly cause eczema itself. Avoiding the trigger food can help to improve or prevent a 'flare-up', but it will not necessarily completely cure the eczema. Allergy testing in this situation with no other allergy symptoms is inaccurate and should be interpreted with caution by a specialist.

Tips to help

✓ Keep baby's skin well moisturised with emollient creams.*

✓ Ensure daily bathing with tepid water as heat can aggravate eczema.

✓ Use emollients as soap substitutes and avoid baby washes, shampoos or bubble bath.

✓ Treat any eczema flares promptly and adequately with corticosteroid or other anti-inflammatory cream prescribed by your doctor.

✓ Keep baby's nails short or use sleepsuits with mittens to avoid scratching.

✓ Aim for a cool room temperature of around 18°C.

*Some research has shown that regular moisturising of children who don't have eczema was associated with an increased risk of food allergies so it is best to only apply emollients if your child suffers with eczema or a skin condition where you have been advised to by a doctor.

When to introduce allergens

As discussed earlier, your baby should start solids when they are developmentally ready, regardless of whether they are at high or low risk of developing allergies (and, most importantly, not before four months). Some babies may already have food allergies, especially if they are towards one end of the spectrum with severe eczema. It is reassuring that the risk of a severe reaction (anaphylaxis) is actually quite low and happens in approximately 1–2 per 1,000 babies. You may want to chat to your family doctor before introducing egg and peanut if your baby does have severe eczema or food allergies. It can help to talk through the benefits of allergy testing at this age versus the risk of delaying allergy introduction while waiting for any testing to be carried out by a specialist.

BABY AT HIGHER RISK OF FOOD ALLERGY
Baby has eczema (early onset or moderate to severe) OR already has a food allergy

→ When your baby is ready, introduce solid foods including egg and peanut **from around four months** followed by other foods known to cause food allergies.

BABY NOT AT HIGH RISK OF FOOD ALLERGY
But someone in the household has a food allergy

→ Carefully plan introducing the allergen; **do not delay introducing past 12 months.**

ALL OTHER BABIES
When your baby is ready

→ **At around six months**, introduce solid foods including peanuts, egg or other food allergens that you and your family eat as part of your normal diet.

What does an allergic reaction look like?

There are different types of allergic reactions which can cause lots of confusion among parents/caregivers, and can even be a challenge to diagnose by a healthcare professional. Allergic reactions are broadly classified into two categories, depending on how the immune system reacts to the allergen:

1. **Immediate reactions:**
   where symptoms can appear quickly, within minutes of ingestion.

2. **Delayed reactions:**
   where symptoms can develop around 2 hours and up to 72 hours later.

Both reactions require a focused allergy history from your doctor and will be subsequently managed according to the type.

Immediate reactions

Immediate reactions can be further divided into mild to moderate reactions or severe reactions. Mild to moderate reactions are those with non-life-threatening symptoms, such as mild facial swelling, rashes or vomiting. In these situations, you can contact your family doctor for advice (on the day ideally) and stop the causative food in the meantime. An open discussion with your doctor about a referral to an allergy specialist for allergy testing should be had. If you are not satisfied with the outcome, it is always worth going back for another chat to ensure you have had the chance to advocate for your child and address any worries. (We know 90% of babies with food allergies don't get to see anyone other than their family doctor.)

Severe reactions are potentially life-threatening and are known as anaphylaxis. It can be helpful to remember the symptoms as 'ABC' which stands for 'Airway, Breathing and Circulation.' **Airway symptoms** include swelling in the throat, tongue and/or upper airways (throat tightening, hoarse voice, difficulty swallowing). **Breathing symptoms** to look for are sudden onset wheezing, breathing difficulty and/or noisy breathing. **Circulation problems** can present as dizziness, feeling faint, sudden sleepiness, confusion, pale clammy skin and loss of consciousness. Although anaphylaxis is rare, it occurs very quickly and requires immediate and urgent medical care. The emergency services should be called and your child will be taken to hospital for further assessment. Once your child is stable and well, a referral to an allergy specialist should be discussed on discharge from the hospital and the allergen should be strictly avoided. Current guidance recommends babies with anaphylaxis or multiple allergies should be under a specialist team.

Immediate type food allergy

MILD TO MODERATE	SEVERE
Swollen lips, face, eyes, itchy rash, hives, urticaria, abdominal pain, vomiting	(ABC) Airway – swelling in the throat, tongue and/or upper airways (throat tightening, hoarse voice, difficulty swallowing). Breathing – sudden onset wheezing, breathing difficulty and/or noisy breathing Circulation – dizziness, feeling faint, sudden sleepiness, confusion, pale clammy skin and loss of consciousness

Call your family doctor in hours or the out-of-hours team for advice (111 in the UK).

Avoid the causative food.

Discuss a possible referral to an allergy specialist.

Call the emergency services for an ambulance (999 in the UK).

Discuss referral to an allergy specialist on discharge.

Immediate type reactions and eczema

A baby with an immediate allergic reaction may develop a sudden flare of eczema. If you think your baby has a food allergy, keep a food diary to note down any reactions and speak with your family doctor. They may suggest a trial of eliminating a trigger food, but caution should be taken. Avoid changing your child's diet unless recommended by a healthcare professional as it may unnecessarily affect your baby's nutritional intake, growth and development. If you are breastfeeding, then consuming an allergen in your diet such as egg may also flare eczema if your child is allergic to it. After a period of elimination, you may then be advised to reintroduce the trigger food if safe to do so back into your/your baby's diet or a referral to a dermatologist or paediatric allergist may be necessary.

Delayed reactions

Delayed reactions can be harder to recognise as symptoms are often vague and don't necessarily occur straight away after consumption of the allergen. It is also easy to dismiss symptoms as perhaps a viral illness. With delayed reactions, symptoms don't tend to be life-threatening, but nevertheless are still bothersome, including gastrointestinal irritation such as abdominal pain, vomiting, a change in bowel habit or skin reactions such as rashes or worsening eczema. Reassuringly, delayed food allergies cannot trigger anaphylaxis like immediate reactions can.

Whilst we don't want to be over-diagnosing children with food allergies (as this would not be in their best interest), if you have concerns regarding your baby's growth and/or they are showing signs of reflux, gut symptoms, food refusal or worsening eczema, chat it through with your doctor. There are a host of non-allergy related conditions that can be responsible but if symptoms are severe, persistent, multiple and/or treatment-resistant then a referral to a specialist allergy clinic may be needed for clarity. This is especially if there is ongoing doubt about the diagnosis. Often, it takes a long time for people with delayed reactions to get the help they need, so it's really important to advocate for your child if you feel something is being missed.

Delayed type food allergy
Symptoms occur within several hours of food trigger

GUT SYMPTOMS
recurrent abdominal pain, vomiting, reflux, food refusal or aversion, loose or frequent stools (six to eight times per day) or constipation (infrequent stools two or fewer per week)

SKIN SYMPTOMS
skin reddening or itching all over the body, worsening eczema

Speak to an appropriate healthcare professional for advice.
If advised to, stop suspected food and symptoms should resolve within a few days.

IF SYMPTOMS ARE NOT SEVERE
consider reintroducing the food one to two weeks later.

IF SYMPTOMS RECUR OR ARE SEVERE OR YOUR CHILD IS NOT GROWING
discuss with your family doctor or consider an allergy specialist referral.

The National Institute for Health and Care Excellence (NICE) recommends referral to a specialist clinic if there is faltering growth, reflux or gut symptoms, food refusal or eczema which worsens with specific foods.

Contact reactions

A contact reaction – also known as contact dermatitis – occurs when your baby's skin reacts to a particular food it has been in contact with. Certain foods are more likely to cause this, such as citrus fruits, tomatoes, berries and histamine-rich foods such as spinach or aubergine. The reaction is extremely common and generally harmless in isolation and does not mean your baby has a food allergy. It can be helpful to take photos of the rash and keep a food symptom diary. Avoid the irritant food for several days. If in doubt about a food allergy, do not reintroduce it and speak to your family doctor for advice. They may suggest using a barrier cream, such as Vaseline, around the mouth if it is thought to be a harmless contact reaction, and the food can be reintroduced safely back into your child's diet. Children tend to eventually grow out of contact reactions as their skin matures and becomes less sensitive.

How to spot a contact reaction versus an allergic reaction

	CONTACT REACTION	**ALLERGIC REACTION**
AREA	Contact area with food (e.g. mouth, chin, cheeks)	Rash spreads to other areas of the body that food has not been in contact with.
RASH	Self-resolves quickly after food is wiped away.	Raised, red and itchy (hives) and may last a short while or persist for hours.
SYMPTOM	No associated symptoms and baby is otherwise fully well, happy and alert.	Associated symptoms such as runny nose, watery eyes, wheezing, coughing, vomiting, unwell or signs of anaphylaxis.

Food allergy or not?

There are some conditions which we often talk about that get very muddled, not only among parents/caregivers but also healthcare professionals, due to the similarities in how they present. Some of them *are* a type of food allergy and some of them are a completely different condition altogether, unrelated to allergy. Below I have outlined a brief definition of common conditions so that if you hear your healthcare professional talking about these terms, you can easily distinguish between whether they are an allergy or not.

Cow's milk protein allergy (CMPA)

CMPA occurs when the immune system reacts to a protein found in cow's milk. CMPA is one of the most common food allergies affecting 1-2 per cent of babies. However, a large proportion will outgrow this. Although some of the symptoms overlap with lactose intolerance (which we'll explore below), occasionally CMPA can be life-threatening so it is important to know the difference between the two. Babies with CMPA cannot consume lactose-free milk as it still contains the cow's milk protein that they are allergic to, and they will need to avoid all dairy products. Depending on the type of reaction, you may be asked to remove the food from your baby's diet and referred to a specialist for allergy testing if there is an immediate reaction. If your baby is classed as having a delayed allergy, you may be asked to keep a symptom diary, remove dairy and then reintroduce it after two to four weeks to confirm the diagnosis. It can be hard to determine if it is a food allergy or another condition, so it is best not to exclude any foods from your baby's diet in the long term without the guidance of a healthcare professional.

Lactose intolerance

Lactose intolerance is an inability to digest a sugar (lactose) found in cow's milk. While it can cause great discomfort, reassuringly it is not life-threatening nor an allergy. Lactose intolerance is rare in babies and toddlers. However, if it occurs, your baby can safely consume lactose-free milk products to relieve the symptoms.

Lactose intolerance can commonly occur in children following gastroenteritis and is referred to as 'secondary lactose intolerance'. This is temporary and will usually get better within six to eight weeks. It may be best to avoid dairy during this time and reintroduce it into the diet gradually. The confusion between CMPA and lactose intolerance is common because what we now know as 'delayed CMPA' used to be referred to as cow's milk intolerance which would often blur the lines.

Coeliac disease

Coeliac disease is when the immune system mistakenly attacks healthy tissues when gluten is consumed, causing damage to the gut lining. This is known as an 'autoimmune' disease rather than a food allergy. Coeliac disease can prevent the body being able to properly absorb lots of different nutrients. It will only present itself once you have introduced gluten into your baby's diet. Gluten is found in all foods containing wheat, barley and rye. The condition can run in families and affects around 1 in 100 people in the UK. However, many people remain undiagnosed as the symptoms can be vague. The condition is lifelong, and the only way to prevent long-term complications is to sustain a strict gluten-free diet. If a first-degree relative (such as a parent or sibling) suffers with coeliac disease, current guidance recommends testing children, which is usually in the form of a blood test. It is essential not to remove gluten from your baby's diet until they have been tested as it will affect the result.

Wheat allergy

Wheat allergy occurs when the immune system reacts to proteins found in wheat when it is eaten and is a separate condition to coeliac disease. Many children with wheat allergy will usually outgrow it by the age of 12. The EAT study showed that babies who were introduced to wheat during the four- to six-month window were less likely to develop coeliac disease at the age of three, but this study only looked at breastfed babies and there is very limited information on this topic. We need more research before we are able to make any recommendations on this.

Food Protein-Induced Enterocolitis Syndrome (FPIES)

This is an uncommon, delayed allergic reaction to a food or formula which leads to repeated vomiting and gastrointestinal symptoms one to six hours after it has been eaten. Symptoms often last for one to two hours only. Sometimes, FPIES can lead to dehydration and other blood pressure or temperature changes. Common food triggers are cow's milk, soy, rice, oats, egg and certain fruits/vegetables. FPIES can be difficult to diagnose as it may look like food poisoning or gastroenteritis. In formula-fed babies, it can cause ongoing watery or bloody diarrhoea, colic, episodes of vomiting and weight loss. Symptoms can take several days or weeks to fully settle after removing the food from the diet. It is unclear why, but FPIES is extremely rare in exclusively breastfed infants. Most children will outgrow FPIES by the age of two.

> ### Who needs allergy testing?
>
> Not everyone with a suspected allergy will need allergy testing, and it is important to discuss this with your healthcare professional who can decide if there is any benefit. Some of the tests, such as skin prick testing, can cause a 'false positive', meaning it is incorrectly positive which can confuse things even more. If your baby has a delayed type allergy, a negative skin prick test does not necessarily mean there is no food allergy; it may just mean it is not an immediate type allergy. The story around the symptoms and reaction to a food are sometimes far more important than any test. This is why it can be useful to write things down and take pictures during a reaction to show your doctor and help work out what is going on.

Outgrowing allergies

It can feel very overwhelming if your child is diagnosed with a food allergy, or any long-term condition for that matter, causing worry for their future and how you will keep them safe. The good news is that most children with an allergy to cow's milk, wheat, soy and hens' eggs will outgrow their allergy during childhood, usually by the age of five. For some children (approximately one in five), allergies will persist into adulthood. There are some food allergies which are less likely to be outgrown, such as peanuts, tree nuts, fish and shellfish, although approximately 30 per cent of children with a sesame or fish allergy, 20 per cent of children with a peanut allergy and 10 per cent of children with a tree nut allergy will outgrow their allergy by the age of five. The most accurate way to find out if a child has outgrown an allergy is through regular allergy testing under a specialist. Online allergy or intolerance tests, which are mostly being marketed for children aged two and over, are usually expensive and can be inaccurate so should not be relied upon.

We have covered a lot of information in this chapter – from the basic principles of weaning and choosing the right approach for your family to building balanced meals, things to watch out for and a whole section on navigating allergies. I hope you are starting to feel like you understand the process of weaning better and what the end goals are. My aim in writing this chapter is to help you to feel more confident when starting out on your baby's weaning journey, empowering you to make the right decisions for you and your family, and teaching you how to keep your baby safe while simplifying as much as possible so it does not feel so daunting.

In the next chapter, we will discuss getting started with weaning, looking at any equipment you might need, and how much and when to feed your child. We will also look at some of the common issues I get asked about in practice, as well as how to handle any setbacks you might encounter along the way.

Getting Started

CHAPTER 2

This chapter is all about the practical aspects of weaning, including any equipment you might need and how exactly to introduce solids, prepare finger foods and progress through textures. One of the most common questions I hear from parents/caregivers is around schedules, such as when to increase meals and how to maintain a schedule, so I have also touched on this along with offering some sample routines to help guide you at each stage of weaning. There are also lots of tips on food storage, eating out, cutlery, cup drinking and much more, as well as a really useful section on handling setbacks, which covers topics I often see in my clinic, and some tips on managing your own anxieties. I truly hope that this information will help you to confidently work through any challenges you might face at home and help you to know when to seek further advice.

Before we get started, it can be helpful to organise what equipment you might need at home ...

GETTING STARTED

Equipment You'll Need

With all the weaning products on the market, it can feel a little overwhelming to figure out what is necessary, so below is my checklist of 'essentials' to help prepare you before you start.

Essential equipment

HIGHCHAIR:

A simple design that is easy to clean is a bonus as weaning can get messy! Make sure your baby can stay sitting up either independently or supported with a cushion. Their hips, knees and ankles should be at 90-degree angles to promote stability. Ideally, their feet should be supported to help with coordination as opposed to dangling in the air. If your highchair doesn't have a footrest, you can improvise by wrapping something, such as an exercise band, around the legs of the highchair at the necessary level for your baby to rest their feet on.

BIBS:

My top tip is for babies to always wear two different types of bibs – a long-sleeved one for coverage from spills, which your baby would typically wear as an 'apron', and a 'catch' bib which is the traditional style of bib that fastens around the neck with a wide base to help collect food that is dropped (and reduce wastage if you want to pop it back on the highchair table).

GETTING STARTED

SUCTION BOWLS/ PLATES:

Suction bowls and plates are great at staying stuck down to the highchair table (until babies learn how to pull them off, that is!). More environmentally-friendly options include silicone or bamboo which will not break if they are dropped; however, you don't have to buy something new if you don't want to. During the earlier stages of weaning, you may just want to put food straight on the highchair table, which is absolutely fine.

BABY CUTLERY:

You can start with flexible cutlery such as silicone to make it more comfortable on your baby's gums and eventually progress to metal (bear in mind that metal can absorb heat from food). Shorter utensils which have a textured grip may be easier for your baby to hold which can help them to practise self-feeding. Some babies may prefer to hold longer utensils (like my youngest) so try different options to see what works for your little one.

FIRST CUP:

Dentists recommend open cups or free-flowing, non-valved sippy cups for oral health (see page 92 for more on introducing a cup). They don't have to be expensive or branded – a small food storage pot can even double up as a mini open cup.

SPLASH MAT:

Choose an easy-to-clean mat that can go in the washing machine if needed and it will save you having to constantly mop the floor. If the splash mat is clean, you can also pick up food that has fallen onto it to avoid wastage.

REUSABLE CLOTHS OR WIPES:

For wiping down faces, hands and equipment at the end of a meal. (Avoid wiping your baby during the meal as it can lead to negative associations.) Alternatively, I like to dunk little hands and feet in tepid water in a bowl or under the tap if it has been a particularly messy session, then give them a dry with a soft towel.

Optional extras

There are lots of beautiful weaning accessories on the market, but it really does not need to be more complicated than the products I've listed above. However, if you want to invest in extra utensils to make the cooking process easier, you may want to consider the following:

STEAMER:	To help steam and soften any vegetables or fruit. This can help retain more of the nutrients versus boiling.
BLENDER:	Essential if you want to make purées or smoothies. A hand blender can work well – it doesn't have to be huge and fancy.
PEELER:	To easily and safely remove tough skins off fruit and vegetables.
MASHER:	Can be easier than using a fork, for example to mash an avocado or banana. If you want to offer purées but keep some texture then a masher is perfect.
CRINKLE CUTTER:	Not only does it make food look pretty, but, functionally, it makes it easier for your baby to hold by providing some grip due to the crinkled edges.
STORAGE POTS OR TUPPERWARE:	For storing food in the fridge or freezer when batch cooking and will generally make your life easier when out and about.
ICE CUBE TRAYS:	For freezing small amounts of food, such as purées, which can then be defrosted one cube at a time instead of defrosting the whole batch.

Note that sterilisation is not needed once your baby is six months old, so any equipment can simply be cleaned in hot, soapy water.

GETTING STARTED

Weaning in Practice

I know that getting started with weaning can feel overwhelming, so in this section I've broken things down for you and we'll look at everything from what time of day to first introduce solids, what and how much to offer and what to do about snacks, to progressing through textures and how to prepare finger foods.

What time of day?

Aim to start with one meal a day so you and your baby can gradually get used to solids. There is no specific time of day that a first meal has to be given – pick the mealtime when you are not rushing and are largely free from distractions to keep the environment calm. You also want to ensure you have time to serve and prepare food beforehand (as well as clean up afterwards!). Think about the time of day when your baby seems to be in the best mood and isn't overtired or due a nap. For many, this may be after they wake up from their first nap and have had a milk feed – approximately 11am. While you are offering first tastes, it doesn't matter too much if the time is a little variable (you may need to experiment to find a time that suits you both). However, once you are offering a meal, sticking to the same time each day can help your baby learn what to expect and may help you fall into a routine.

What about first tastes?

There is some research to suggest that introducing bitter flavours such as vegetables early on when starting solids and consistently exposing your baby to them can increase their acceptance of vegetables until at least 12 months, and potentially thereafter. Below are some suggestions for introducing vegetables to your baby, and the box on the next page explains how to serve them. Of course, you don't need to start your baby on vegetables if, culturally, you don't feel it is appropriate or you have other foods in mind.

Here is an example of what introducing vegetables as first tastes might look like in the early days:

> **DAY 1**
> Broccoli floret + broccoli purée
>
> **DAY 2**
> Cauliflower floret + cauliflower purée
>
> **DAY 3**
> Courgette spear + courgette purée
>
> **DAY 4**
> Avocado spear + mashed avocado
>
> **DAY 5**
> Green beans + green bean purée
>
> **DAY 6**
> Parsnip batons + parsnip purée

If your baby is enthusiastic from the get-go and there seems to be more than a few mouthfuls going in, I would move on to offering iron-rich and more energy-dense foods to ensure low-calorie vegetables are not displacing the nutrients they are getting from milk. This happened with my firstborn and his rate of growth slowed during the first month of weaning. I wish I had had the confidence at the time to introduce other foods more quickly, but I was unsure how to move on from first tastes to family meals. This is why I have included transition meals in Part Two to make things easier for you (see page 122) and have also included a section on page 78 on progressing through textures.

How to serve vegetables

STEP 1:
Wash the vegetable thoroughly, then cut it into large pieces so it can be easily picked up by your baby.

STEP 2:
Steam or boil the vegetable (steaming helps to retain more of the nutrients) until it can squish on gentle pressure between your finger and thumb.

STEP 3:
Rinse the cooked veg in cool water if you need to cool it down quickly.

STEP 4:
If you are baby-led weaning, you can offer one or two pieces to your baby now. If you are spoon-feeding, blend the pieces in a blender with some of your baby's usual milk or water to your desired consistency. If you are combination feeding, take out one piece to serve as finger food (and remove any you may want to serve to the rest of the family) before puréeing the remaining pieces.

STEP 5:
Offer the purée (on a pre-loaded spoon) or both the finger food and purée to your baby and watch them enjoy pulling funny faces!

For vegetables that don't need to be cooked, such as avocado, peel and de-stone half an avocado, before slicing some of it into spears and mashing the remaining avocado until you have a smooth consistency.

How much food to offer?

It is completely normal for parents/caregivers to spend lots of time worrying about how much solid food their baby is consuming. I want to reassure you that there are no definitive guidelines on solid food amounts between 6 and 12 months as there is such a variation of what is 'normal'. Your baby will simply need small portions to begin with, so try to serve only what you need to avoid food wastage. If your baby still seems hungry, you can always top up with more food.

Focus on feeding your baby 'responsively' – look out for their signals, just as you would with milk, rather than focusing on a specific portion size or volume to avoid under- or overfeeding your baby. Babies are good at self-regulating and, if you pay close attention at mealtimes, you will start to recognise your baby's individual cues (signals) and learn when they have had enough. This may change along the way as they develop new skills such as windscreen wiping the highchair or throwing their plate on the floor!

GETTING STARTED

HUNGER CUES:
- May be more alert and active
- Excited while looking at food
- Opens mouth towards food
- Uses hand motions or sounds reaches for food

FULLNESS CUES:
- Slows pace of feeding
- Turns head away from food
- Closes mouth towards food
- Uses hand motions or sounds
- Pushes food away or windscreen wipes the table

SIGNS BABY IS GETTING ENOUGH FOOD:
- Periods of being content/playful
- Several wet nappies a day
- Regular bowel movements (although weaning can initially cause constipation as the digestive system adapts to solids – see page 108 for advice on this)
- Gaining weight and following their centile on the growth chart

If you are watching out for your baby's cues and responding to their needs accordingly, it is likely they are having exactly what they need and there is no need to worry. However, if you have any concerns regarding your little one's intake, please speak to your family doctor or health visitor for more tailored advice (also see page 104 for more advice on babies who are slow to wean).

6 months

When starting solids, try not to worry if not much food is going in to begin with. It's more about getting your baby used to different tastes and textures, and allowing them to practise their hand–eye coordination. Starting solids can be overwhelming to the senses, so try to give your baby some time to get to grips with weaning and avoid putting any pressure on them. If they seem unhappy, remove them from the highchair and try again tomorrow. Milk amounts should not significantly change at the start. If your baby seems very keen and is gobbling up all their food and gesturing for more, just be sure to offer their milk before solids so milk is not being displaced too quickly. All breastfed babies should take a vitamin A and C supplement from 6 months and a vitamin D supplement from birth (it is not too late to start – see page 34).

7–9 months

During this period, you will gradually notice more of a shift towards solid foods as your baby's feeding skills start to progress. When your little one is confidently eating one meal per day, you can then add in a second meal and so on until they are having three meals a day (breakfast, lunch and dinner). This will be in addition to their usual milk feeds. However, they may reduce milk at each feed or drop one entirely as their solid intake increases. Some babies can be on three meals just after seven months and others may not be ready for three meals until they are closer to nine months. Move at your baby's pace and try your hardest not to compare to others – each baby is on their own journey (this includes sibling comparison).

According to current guidance, formula-fed babies will be consuming approximately 600ml of milk per day (don't worry if this is a little more or a little less than your baby is having – it is just a guide!). It can be difficult to quantify milk intake while breastfeeding; however, babies will usually adapt feeds according to their solid intake. Start with offering milk first then solids approximately 60 minutes after feeds. It is worth noting that some babies might want a bit of milk in their tummies to happily come to the table rather than being over-hungry. Others may need longer than 60 minutes between their milk feed and solids if they consistently don't appear to have much of an appetite.

Gradually increase the quantity and range of food offered to ensure your baby has the best opportunity to gain all the energy and nutrients they need. Cup-drinking skills will gradually improve as your baby continues to practice and becomes more confident.

10–12 months

At this stage, most babies will have moved to three meals a day (breakfast, lunch and dinner) and may have dropped to approximately three milk feeds per day. As a rough guide, formula-fed babies will drink about 400ml per day at this stage. If your little one is drinking significantly more milk than this and is not increasing their solid intake, then you can consider reducing milk to see if it helps and consistently offering solids before milk. Breastfed babies will continue to adapt their milk consumption as their food intake changes. It is common for babies to lose interest in milk between nine and twelve months. If this happens, don't panic and try to offer milk in a distraction-free zone with limited noise and dim lighting before solid meals (albeit this is difficult when out and about!). Babies should be enjoying a wide range of flavours and different textures during this time while picking up finger foods and moving them to their mouth.

Formula-fed babies should take a vitamin supplement if they are consuming less than 500ml of milk per day (see page 36).

Over 12 months

You might feel your baby is 'weaned' by this point, and hopefully they are happily sharing family meals, but there are likely to be some adjustments in place still. The emphasis here is to continue to build on the foundations of their feeding skills by offering a variety of textures and flavours. You may feel ready to stop modifying some foods, such as squishing berries, or you may want to offer some appropriately sliced raw fruits and veggies. Starting solids is an ongoing process and handling more challenging textures is not something that will happen overnight, but you will get a sense of when your baby is ready for the next steps – for example, offering them a banana whole as opposed to breaking it up. There is absolutely no rush and you may prefer to wait until your child is older to introduce higher risk foods, as discussed on page 46. Your baby may be showing more enthusiasm for cutlery at this age, and they can practise scooping food with a spoon independently and putting it to their mouth (see page 94 for more on introducing cutlery).

Should I offer water to my baby?

Before six months, you don't need to introduce water if you are exclusively breastfeeding. Even on a hot day, studies have shown that breastfed babies do not need any extra fluids but may naturally breastfeed more frequently if needed. If you are formula-feeding, the current advice is for your baby to have sips of cool boiled water only after milk feeds if it is a particularly hot day. Babies drinking exclusively expressed milk may require more breast milk, and combination feeding babies may require more breastfeeds.

After six months, water does not need to be boiled and cooled in the UK. Sips of water are encouraged with meals to practise cup-drinking skills and to introduce the taste (see page 92 for more on introducing a cup). On a hot day, again you can offer water after milk feeds, more so for formula-fed babies as breastfed babies may increase their feeds accordingly.

Progressing through textures

If you choose to begin your baby's weaning journey with purées alone, and finger foods are not for you and your baby, I want to offer some tips to try to prevent your baby getting stuck on one consistency. You may even have started weaning and now want to find a way to progress through textures, in which case you are in the right place.

The aim is for your baby to eventually be sharing family meals with lots of different textures to avoid having to cook different meals, which only makes life more hectic. The same family meal can be served slightly differently to baby (for example, mashed) as their feeding skills develop, but, ideally, you want to get to the stage where only small adjustments are needed to modify their food.

You can control the texture of food by the amount of breast milk, infant formula or water you add to smooth it out. Adding more liquid will give a runnier texture and less liquid will keep it thicker. You can also pulse food in the blender just a couple of times to retain a thicker or lumpy texture. If you don't own a blender, you can mash certain foods, such as avocado, banana and cooked potato, with a fork and control the consistency by mashing it less.

If you start with a smooth liquid purée and find your baby is taking to it quite easily, don't hesitate to move on to a lumpier texture. If they are gagging with every bite, you may wish to continue with purées until they get to grips with it. Once you feel they are able to handle the texture, you can move on to the next one – of course, they may still gag once in a while, but that's perfectly normal. The aim is to progress from smooth to lumpy or mashed food then eventually to minced and chopped food.

Textures

smooth → lumpy → minced → chopped

Traditionally, you may have heard this referred to as different 'stages' of weaning, in which babies start with stage one foods from six months (usually purées) then move on to lumpy foods from seven months (stage two) and build up to mashed or chopped foods by nine to ten months (stage three). We have largely moved away from this now for many reasons, including the introduction of finger foods and baby-led weaning where chopped foods, such as avocado, may be given from the get-go. Sticking rigidly to these stages can feel restrictive to babies who may be able to move through textures more quickly. However, it can still be helpful to think of textures in this way if you are exclusively spoon-feeding and want to gradually transition. I would still encourage the introduction of soft finger foods as part of texture progression as soon as you feel ready.

The speed at which your baby moves through textures will be child-dependent and how comfortable you are during the weaning process to move forwards. There is thought to be an optimum window between six and nine months when babies may find it easiest to learn how to chew, manoeuvre and swallow food. This is not to say that your baby can't learn these skills after this time, but it may take a little longer, particularly if they have only had exposure to one type of smooth texture.

Some children may just naturally take longer to accept finger foods or lumpier textures (see page 104 for more on babies who are slow to wean). However, if you are concerned that after nine to ten months your little one will still not engage with any finger foods or textured food, please seek advice from your health visitor or family doctor who may be able to refer you for further support.

A word on pouches

Offering your baby pouches may help to boost your confidence at the start of introducing solids. Pouches can be added into a meal with finger foods such as pasta or soft vegetables. They can also be beneficial when travelling on long journeys or on aeroplanes as we all know it is not realistic to always carry pre-prepared food all the time. However, the downside is that they often offer just one type of texture. As we've seen, the aim is to expose your baby to a variety of different textures and flavours, which would be difficult to achieve if they are consuming pouches at every meal during their weaning journey.

When choosing a pouch, pick a savoury option over a fruit one and vary the texture where possible. Fruit pouches (blended fruit) contain lots of 'free sugars' that are not ideal for dental health if given frequently and may lead to your baby consuming more sugar than if eating the actual solid fruit itself. Avoid letting your baby suck straight from the pouch to prevent tooth decay.

How to prepare finger foods

If you choose the baby-led weaning route and would prefer to offer your baby finger foods from the get-go, you need to make sure they are as safe as can be for your baby.

At around six months, finger foods are usually sticks of soft food, roughly the size of your finger in length. The sticks of food need to be wide enough for your baby to grasp, but narrow enough for them to close their whole hand around it with their palmer grasp (picking things up with their fingers and palm). The texture of the food should ideally be firm enough for baby to pick up, but soft enough to squish easily between your finger and thumb with gentle pressure. Based on this, overcooked veggies tend to be good options or soft, overripe fruits (see the examples below). If foods are too slippery, such as avocado fingers, then you can roll them in oats or flaxseed to make them easier to grasp. Overcooked pasta and unsalted buttered toast fingers are also great options as are oat fingers, pancakes and fritters.

At around nine months, your baby will start to develop the pincer grasp where they are able to pick something up with their thumb and forefinger. This means it is safe to cut soft food up into small pieces for them to pick up and eat. These finger foods might be a similar consistency and texture to above to begin with or your baby may have progressed to slightly firmer foods, such as less ripe fruits or less overcooked vegetables/pasta. Keep trying to gradually transition so your baby can not only develop their feeding skills, but learn to enjoy similar foods to you without having to adjust them too much.

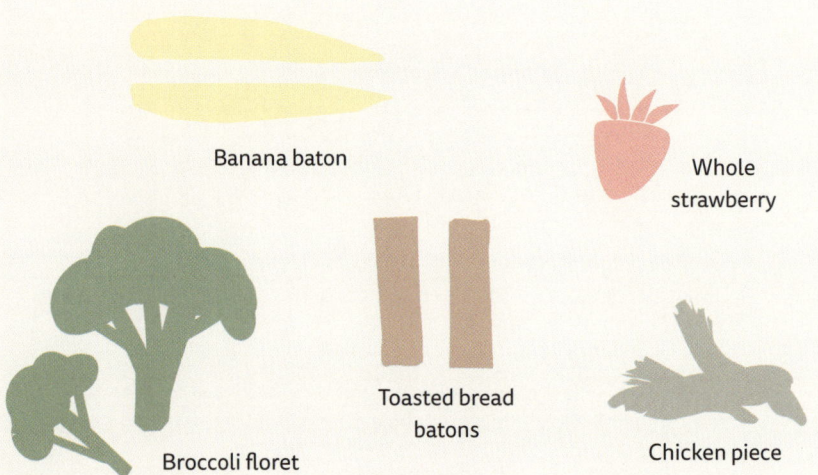

When to introduce snacks

Current guidance recommends that snacks are introduced to your little one at around 12 months of age. If your baby is under 12 months and is still hungry between meals, it is generally advised to offer extra milk feeds between meals in the first instance as it is still an important source of nutrition before the age of one. Once your baby is closer to one, you can introduce two healthy snacks between meals, or you can take a gradual approach and try one snack first to gauge how it impacts mealtimes, then add a second (see the schedule on the next page).

The best way to view snacks is as mini meals with an opportunity to boost nutrition. However, snacks should not replace meals. Relatively speaking, one snack should make up approximately 10 per cent of your little one's total daily intake. It can be hard to measure this and there will be some children who will be able to eat lots of snacks and still gobble up all their meals; and there will be others who have a snack and then may have no interest in their next meal. Remember, this is just a rough guide and it can take a bit of trial and error to get the portion size right for your child. My advice is to start small with snacks and slowly increase the amounts. As babies have small stomachs, giving them extra opportunities to eat can be beneficial, but it does not mean that every opportunity will result in food consumption.

Sample weaning schedule

You have probably just got your head around milk feeds, naps and bedtime, and then all of a sudden you are adding in solids and wondering where this is going to fit into your schedule. On another note, if you aren't in any sort of routine yet (which many of us aren't, as you may still be working out your baby's optimum feeding and sleeping habits or just going with the flow), then I have always found that transitioning to solids is a great way to build a routine if you are looking for one. I have offered some sample routines below, more for reassurance, but remember they are just a guide and there will be some give and take depending on your individual baby and the specific needs of your family. You may incorporate milk into your nap time routine before baby falls asleep, in which case they may not need a milk feed afterwards.

	SIX MONTHS	SEVEN TO NINE MONTHS	TEN TO ELEVEN MONTHS	TWELVE TO EIGHTEEN MONTHS
MORNING 07.00	milk	milk	milk	milk (optional)
08.00			BREAKFAST	BREAKFAST
09.30	nap 1, milk on waking	nap 1, milk on waking	nap 1	SNACK 1
11.30	FIRST TASTES	LUNCH	LUNCH	LUNCH
12.30	nap 2	nap 2	nap 2	nap 1
15.00	milk	milk	milk	SNACK 2
16.00	nap 3	nap 3		
17.00	milk	DINNER	DINNER	DINNER
BEDTIME 19.00–19.30	milk	milk	milk	milk (optional)

GETTING STARTED

How to Introduce Allergens

Whenever I mention introducing allergens to parents/caregivers in my role as a GP, it is usually the first they have heard of it and, of course, there is very limited time to discuss it in the level of detail I'd like during a ten-minute consultation. I therefore wanted to include advice here explaining how to introduce common allergens into your baby's diet to reduce the risk of them developing an allergy to that food.

While more than 170 foods can cause reactions in people with food allergies, there are 9 allergens responsible for 90 per cent of all food allergy reactions: egg, peanuts, cow's milk, tree nuts (such as cashews, almonds and walnuts), wheat, soy, fish, shellfish and sesame seeds.

GETTING STARTED

After completing first tastes, when introducing allergens to your baby, the general advice below may help you to do so safely:

Introduce early in the day: this makes sure there is plenty of time for you to monitor for a reaction and speak to your family doctor within working hours if you do need any advice.

Ensure your baby is well: if your baby is unwell, it might be hard to tell the difference between allergy symptoms and symptoms related to illness, such as rashes. Being unwell may also increase your baby's risk of a more severe reaction to food.

Start with small quantities: you can try offering ¼–½ teaspoon then waiting 10–15 minutes to look for any signs of an immediate reaction. If there is no reaction, you can offer a bit more.

Introduce one allergen at a time: this will help to identify which food is the culprit if your baby does react. You don't need to introduce other foods one at a time as this would reduce the variety of food you can offer your baby before the age of one.

Keep the food within your baby's diet if there is no reaction: this will help to build tolerance and prevent a food allergy developing later (see the next section for more advice on this).

If there is a reaction, stop the allergen immediately: follow the advice on pages 58–59 for next steps.

Below is an example of how to incorporate allergens alongside the first tastes we looked at earlier:

FIRST TASTES	INTRODUCING AN ALLERGEN	CONTINUED EXPOSURE
Day 1 Broccoli floret + broccoli purée	**Day 7** Red pepper slice + mashed egg (hard-boiled egg) (first allergen)	**Day 8** Egg strips + sweet potato (second exposure)
Day 2 Cauliflower floret + cauliflower purée		**Day 9** Butternut squash fingers + pea purée
Day 3 Courgette spear + courgette purée		**Day 10** Avocado fingers + mashed egg (hard-boiled egg) + avocado (third exposure)
Day 4 Avocado spear + mashed avocado		
Day 5 Green beans + green bean purée		
Day 6 Parsnip batons + parsnip purée		

How to offer allergens to your baby

EGG
Hard-boil an egg and mash this with a small amount of breast milk or infant formula to avoid a chalky texture. Offer on the tip of a spoon. You can offer scrambled egg or omelette fingers as long as they are fully cooked, as, if your baby is allergic, they are more likely to have a reaction to uncooked egg.

PEANUTS
Mix 1 teaspoon of nut butter with 2 teaspoons of water and offer a small amount on the tip of a spoon.

COW'S MILK (DAIRY)
Offer natural unsweetened yoghurt on the tip of a spoon.

TREE NUTS
These include cashews, almonds, brazil nuts, hazelnuts, pecans, pistachios, macadamias, shea nuts and walnuts. Mix 1 teaspoon of nut butter with 2 teaspoons of water and offer a small amount on the tip of a spoon or ground in porridge. Introduce each nut separately.

WHEAT
Offer a finger of toast or a teaspoon of a wheat cereal with milk of choice (breast milk, infant formula or dairy if you have introduced it).

SOY
Offer soy yoghurt on the tip of a spoon, a stick of tofu or a small amount of silken tofu blended into sauces or mousses.

FISH (SALMON, HADDOCK, COD)
Offer fully-cooked flaked fish or flake into mash/veg and serve as a lumpy or smooth purée depending on your baby's preference.

SHELLFISH (PRAWNS, MUSSELS, CRAB)
Ensure shellfish is fully cooked and finely chopped before offering. It may also help to mash with potato for texture purposes.

SESAME
Offer home-made hummus (see page 240 for a recipe) on the tip of a spoon or mix 1 teaspoon of tahini with 1 teaspoon of water and offer a small amount.

Maintaining food allergens in the diet

Often, parents/caregivers introduce an allergen into their baby's diet and, if there's no reaction, they naturally think that allergen is ticked off and move on to the next one without coming back to it. However, we do know that it is not just about introducing the allergen, but also about maintaining the allergens within the diet. Offering the allergen two or three times a week can help continue this exposure and may reduce the risk of your baby developing an allergy to it. I know it can be difficult to remember to include all of the foods we've covered above, so, in reality, you may not be able to do this every week with all of them, but you can stir peanut butter into porridge twice a week, for example, and focus on other allergens at lunch and dinner. Below, I have shared a few examples for really simple achievable ideas. There are also lots of meals in Part Two that incorporate all of these ingredients.

- **Egg:** can be hard-boiled, omelette, scrambled, frittata or baked in pancakes/muffins (ensure they are stamped with the British Lion to reduce the risk of salmonella).

- **Peanuts:** peanut butter (on toast), ground into porridge, puffs as finger food or stirred into satay sauce or curry (no whole nuts until over the age of four).

- **Cow's milk (dairy):** natural yoghurt, cheese, cow's milk in cooking or cream in sauces.

- **Tree nuts (cashews, pecans, almonds, walnuts):** ground into porridge, blended into sauces such as pesto or added to baking (no whole nuts until over the age of four).

- **Wheat:** toast, pasta, wheat cereal, couscous or wholemeal flour in baking.

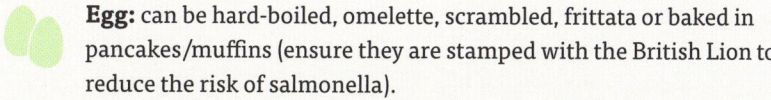

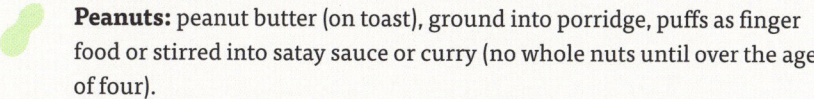

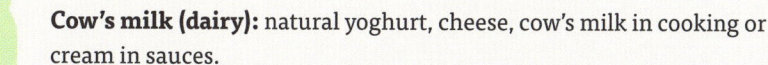

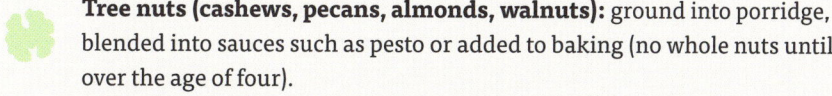

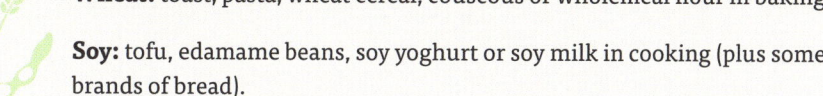

- **Soy:** tofu, edamame beans, soy yoghurt or soy milk in cooking (plus some brands of bread).

- **Fish (salmon, haddock, cod):** home-made fish fingers or fishcakes, mashed into foods such as potato or cooked in a curry or pie.

- **Shellfish (prawns, crab):** ensure it is fully cooked. Prawns can be finely chopped and mashed into other foods.

- **Sesame:** hummus as a dip, tahini added to sauces or ground seeds added to porridge or baking.

Getting Used to Mealtimes

Now that we have covered what foods to serve and how to prepare them, I'd like to focus on the wider aspects of mealtimes to help you and your baby get the most out of them. Mealtimes play an important role in the emotional well-being, and physical and psychological development of our children. We can quickly become laser-focused on nutrition, which, although important, is only one aspect of eating – it is just as important to make eating a fun and relaxed experience, so children feel comfortable and at ease. Weaning is also about so much more than just eating – it is about learning social norms, such as drinking out of a cup, using cutlery and eating out (for those who want to) – and mealtimes provide an opportunity for children to connect to others and strengthen family bonds through communication and a sense of belonging.

When you speak to most dietitians or psychologists, one of the first things they will tell you is to remove pressure at mealtimes as it often backfires. We want children to stay in tune with their hunger and fullness cues (see page 74 for a reminder of these) rather than eating to please us. This is why giving your little one praise when they eat certain amounts or punishments related to not eating are often unhelpful. It is the same for bribing and negotiating as your child gets older – phrases such as 'just one more bite' or 'you can have pudding if you eat all your dinner' may help in the short term, but not in the long term when it comes to developing a healthy relationship with food. We all have days when we resort to these things out of frustration – we are only human – but that's OK, and the important thing is to reflect on it and try again.

We also want children to enjoy mealtimes. Making mess and exploring is part of the learning process when discovering different textures, colours and smells. While I fully empathise that this is not ideal for the grown-ups who have to clear it up, having fun and being in control can help your little one grow in confidence at mealtimes. Some days you won't be able to face it and that's absolutely fine, but when you can, embrace the mess!

Although we are unable to control how much or what foods our little ones eat, there are certainly lots of things we can do to create a positive mealtime environment for our children. Some of my tips may not be realistic for you and your lifestyle, particularly if you are working long hours, but if you can incorporate even one or two into your routine, you may notice a shift towards happier mealtimes. These tips can still apply to toddlers too and continue to be relevant for us even as adults.

GETTING STARTED

GETTING STARTED

My top ten tips for positive mealtimes

1   CREATE A RELAXED ENVIRONMENT

Start with a calm, relaxed environment free from distractions. Gentle music may help. If you have toddler siblings around this isn't always easy and you may choose to start with lunch as your baby's first meal when your toddler might be at childcare or napping.

2   GIVE PRAISE

Focus on praising how your little one is eating – for example, 'Well done on using the spoon' rather than how much they are eating.

3   THINK ABOUT POSITIONING

Reduce overall mealtime stress by ensuring children are seated in a comfortable upright position at a 90-degree angle with their feet supported. This posture enables them to manoeuvre chewing and swallowing more effectively which in turn reduces the risk of choking (see page 44).

4   REDUCE ANXIETY

Try to ensure food is appropriately prepared for your baby's development to reduce the risk of choking and, as a result, your overall anxiety – which can be sensed by little ones. (See page 110 for help with this.)

5   ROLE MODEL

Sit together as a family for meals as much as possible and role model eating the same food while chatting about your day rather than solely focusing on the food. Socialising is a big part of mealtimes that your baby will have observed up until now and will want to be involved in.

6   REMOVE PRESSURE

Avoid pressurising your little one to eat certain foods or finish what is on their plate. Babies are intuitive eaters, so allow them to self-regulate and focus on if their tummy feels 'hungry or full' as they get older. Eating with your baby, even if it is just a little bit of food, helps to take the pressure off them.

7. IMPLEMENT A ROUTINE

Stick to a schedule and ensure milk feeds are not given too close to mealtimes (allow at least a one-hour gap), which will inevitably impact appetite. You may need to do a bit of trial and error as some babies will be happier to sit in their highchair when they aren't over-hungry.

8. AVOID TIREDNESS

Ensure little ones are sufficiently rested – they may not have much patience for the meal if they are overtired and due a nap. The meal itself can be tiring for them, so be mindful of how long they spend in the highchair.

9. GET MESSY

Let your baby explore foods and get messy to learn about textures and tickle their senses. I know the clean-up is tough, and you may not be able to do this three times a day, but the more your baby has the opportunity to explore, the more they will become familiar with a range of different foods. It helps to build independence with food too.

10. OFFER VARIETY

Remember, babies' taste buds are always changing and it can take 10–15 (or more) exposures to a new food before it is accepted, so keep on offering a variety of different foods. It may seem counterintuitive when they are rejecting a food for the tenth time, but if you avoid giving it to them, they will never have the opportunity to learn to like it, which can quickly lead to them accepting a narrow range of foods.

If your baby seems be taking a while to grasp the concept of starting solids and you are several weeks or months into mealtimes with little progress, look back at this list and see if there is anything you can adjust. A common reason babies can be slow to accept solids is because a tweak is needed to their routine – sometimes they just aren't hungry enough after their last milk feed or perhaps they are overtired at the chosen mealtime. You may be doing all of these things and actually there is nothing more you can give your baby other than time (see page 104 for advice on babies who are 'slow to wean').

Remember, you are in control of what foods you offer to your baby, but you are not in control of what they choose to eat or how much, so try your hardest to relax and enjoy mealtimes. It's a great time to connect with your baby and ensure you are also well-fed!

Introducing a cup

There is so much to think about when transitioning to solids that it can be easy to forget about introducing a cup at six months. I know with my firstborn I didn't necessarily make this a priority between the purées and finger foods, which may have added to the challenge we had later down the line. Your baby does not need to be gulping down water at this stage – milk should still be the main drink until the age of one. However, sips of water can be offered to help introduce the taste and to practise their cup-drinking skills.

If your baby isn't showing an interest at first, try not to worry – keep introducing a cup at each meal and demonstrating how to use it. If your baby finds it confusing or distracting at mealtimes, you can wait until the end of the meal if they remain settled in the highchair. I found placing my baby on a splash mat (once they were sitting independently) after a meal was a good opportunity to practise and catch any spillages.

Drinking from a cup is a skill and, like all other skills, requires a lot of practice and encouragement along the way, so patience is key. Some babies will grasp how to do this quite quickly, whereas others may take months and months, which is completely normal. The aim is to try to have them drinking out of a cup by 12 months to help transition from the bottle, if you are using one, to optimise dental health.

What cup to use?

There are a huge number of cups on the market and there isn't one specific cup to recommend. However, there are certain characteristics to look for that are better for oral health. The British Society of Paediatric Dentistry and NHS guidance recommend starting with an open cup as it helps to teach a baby how to sip rather than suck from an early age. Sipping is a developmental necessity that helps to support dental health and plays a pivotal role in jaw and facial development.

If you are out and about, you can offer your baby a cup with a straw for practicality, ideally without a valve so it is free-flowing to prevent your little one from having to suck hard to obtain the water. I appreciate sometimes this is not ideal if knocked over or tipped upside down as it will spill or leak, but it is the best option to help your little one develop the necessary drinking skills. It is worth mentioning that the action of breastfeeding is a completely different oral process from sucking on a drinking cup, so this is absolutely not a reason to end your breastfeeding journey early (unless of course you want to!).

Tips to help with cup drinking

- Start in the highchair at mealtimes to ensure good positioning.
- Put a small amount of liquid in the cup, such as 15–30ml, to keep spills to a minimum.
- Choose a lightweight cup so it's not too heavy for your baby to hold and small enough to put their hands around.
- Help to guide the cup to their mouth with them and, once they get the hang of it, stay nearby in case they need some support.
- Offer lots of praise and positive reinforcement to encourage your baby.
- Let them watch you as babies love to copy and learn through role modelling.

If your baby is still struggling, you can try alternating water with some breast milk or infant formula to see if it helps. Some babies don't naturally love the taste of water and may take time to adjust to it. Equally, some babies don't like certain cups, so you could try a different colour, size or shape to see what works. Finally, if your baby is getting upset with a cup, you could try reintroducing it outside of mealtimes in a less pressured setting, such as during play, to see if it will help them to engage better.

Introducing cutlery

Learning to use cutlery is a complex task and it can take until a child is seven years old on average to successfully use a knife and fork together without being too messy. This requires a lot of patience from caregivers, so don't worry if your little one is only using their hands – there is plenty of time for them to learn!

Self-feeding begins as early as **six months** as babies learn to grasp food (the palmer grasp) and bring it to their mouth. They may also self-feed with a pre-loaded spoon by picking it up from the table or simply being handed it by a caregiver. From around **nine months**, babies tend to develop their pincer grasp where they can self-feed by picking up smaller pieces of food with their thumb and forefinger. You can start to teach them how to use a spoon around this time if they are willing, but most toddlers will be using their hands.

By around **14 months**, babies can usually dip a spoon into food and place it to their mouths (albeit very messily). Eventually, they will learn to scoop with the spoon and, by the age of **two years**, many toddlers want to feed more independently. Between the ages of **two and three**, spoon-feeding skills will continue to develop, and many will be able to stab food with a fork and feed themselves with it. Cutting and spreading with a knife can be practised with child-friendly cutlery from the ages of **three to five years**.

If your baby is not able to use a spoon by the age of two despite role modelling or practising, it's worth having a chat with your family doctor who will carry out a brief assessment and decide if any further support is needed from an occupational therapist.

Around 6 months
May introduce spoon

By 14 months
Often dipping spoon into food & bringing to mouth (messily)

By 24 months
Keen to self-feed with cutlery independently

Tips to help your little one with cutlery

- **Positioning:** lay out the cutlery in the same place for each meal so your baby knows where to find it.

- **Utensils:** think about ease – shorter utensils which are lighter in weight with a textured grip may be easier for your baby to hold initially.

- **Scoopable foods:** yoghurt, porridge or mashed potato are great textures to practise with. Thinner textures such as soups and milk will require deeper spoons, but may be a little more challenging to begin with given their more liquid consistency.

- **Teaching:** all babies learn in different ways, so you may want to try various approaches such as role modelling, guiding them with your hand over their hand as they grasp the spoon or just talking through each step of the process to see what works for your little one.

- **Opportunity:** provide lots of opportunity to practise with guidance. For example, you could see how many peas they can get on their fork to make it fun or if they can make holes in their food to cool it down.

- **Consistency:** make cutlery a part of their routine and try to bring it to the table for every meal.

- **Patience:** developing new skills requires perseverance and it will get messy, but try to stay calm if your little one is accidentally flicking yoghurt all over the walls.

- **Activities:** use utensils between meals in a fun, low-pressure environment such as for cutting up play dough or during meal preparation or role play. You can use child-friendly blunted/non-metal cutlery or a crinkle cutter to help protect little fingers.

2–3 years
Developing spoon & fork skills

3–5 years
Spread/cut with a knife

7 years
Competent with a set of cutlery

*Note: these are averages and do not take into account specific medical conditions

Eating out

At the start of weaning, you might feel more comfortable feeding your baby at home where there are minimal distractions and your little one can really focus on learning how to eat. Once you have found your rhythm, you can certainly enjoy eating out together bearing a few things in mind to make the whole experience easier. This is one of my favourite things to do as I often find while babies are exploring food, they last a little longer in the highchair than toddlers do! It also encourages you to sit with them for longer than you might do at home, which is really lovely bonding time.

Things to pack before you go

- Bib: long-sleeved and/or catch bib to help keep clothes clean

- Plate and cutlery for familiarity

- Pre-prepared food if this makes you feel more comfortable (you may want to heat this up just before you leave so it will be cooled enough when your baby comes to eat it)

- Wipes or disposable cloths for the clean-up

- A separate bag to place bib/plate/cutlery in when you are finished

- Beaker of water

Tips while you are there

- Politely ask your server to help you with a highchair if your hands are full – most will ask you on arrival; accept the help where you can!

- Notify your server of any allergies if your baby will be eating off the menu.

- Children's menus can be very limiting, and you might prefer to order off the adult menu and share a meal together.

- Discuss with your server about avoiding added salt where possible and ensuring your dish does not contain any honey or other foods you would not like your baby to eat (see pages 48–51 for a reminder of foods to avoid).

- If your baby is super hungry, you might want to confirm the wait time on food or whether your baby's food can be prioritised (restaurants are generally happy to bring children's food first, especially if you are with a large party and the mains might take a while to come).

- It is worth waiting until the food has arrived before putting your baby in the highchair, otherwise they may lose the stamina (you can sit your baby on your knee in the meantime or walk around the restaurant to familiarise them with the surroundings).

- You can ask your server if the food can be cooled before bringing it to the table as most babies might try to grab at it or lose patience while waiting for it to cool down.

- It is easy to become distracted when you are out, so be sure to keep an eye on your baby at all times to spot any signs of choking.

How and When to Transition to Cow's Milk

One of the most common questions I am asked by parents/caregivers is how and when to transition their baby from infant formula or breast milk on to cow's milk (or other preferred milk), so I thought I would add in some tips here.

Infant formula-feeding

If your baby is formula-fed, as mentioned in Chapter 1, they no longer need to continue with formula past 12 months unless you have specifically been told to do so by a healthcare professional, such as an allergy specialist. It is a personal choice if you want to switch from formula to cow's milk or a fortified alternative milk that perhaps the whole family already drinks. You may also want to think about transitioning your baby from a bottle to a cup to support their dental health. I would suggest making one change at a time, for example, the type of milk first, then the cup (or vice versa), as it may be too overwhelming for your baby to change everything at once.

Breastfeeding

If you are away from your baby for long periods of time, you may wish to introduce cow's milk (or a fortified alternative milk if preferred) at 12 months in a cup. While your baby is away from you, they can still consume dairy/dairy alternatives to meet their calcium requirements, depending on how much you are breastfeeding outside of this.

Milk refusal

If you are putting your baby into childcare at 12 months and they are refusing to drink cow's milk (or your preferred fortified milk of choice), try not to worry. While some babies can transition overnight, others can take weeks to get used to the taste after only having infant formula or breast milk. Most daycare facilities are accommodating and happy to use specific types of milk, cups or bottles that are accepted by your baby until you have managed to fully transition them, which, in reality, can take months! You can try mixing milks together for a subtle transition over a two-week period (or longer if needed), as follows:

- **Days 1–3:**
  150ml (5oz) formula/breast milk
  + 30ml (1oz) milk of choice

- **Days 4–6:**
  120ml (4oz) formula/breast milk
  + 60ml (2oz) milk of choice

- **Days 7–9:**
  90ml (3oz) formula/breast milk
  + 90ml (3oz) milk of choice

- **Days 10–12:**
  60ml (2oz) formula/breast milk
  + 120ml (4oz) milk of choice

- **Days 12–14:**
  30ml (1oz) formula/breast milk
  + 150ml (5oz) milk of choice

milk of choice

formula/breast milk

My firstborn refused any milk in a cup and never took to a bottle so would only have cow's milk in cereal at nursery, which made me quite anxious when I returned to work. The milk recommendations at present are approximately 350–400ml per day from 12 months – this is the equivalent of 2–3 portions of dairy (such as yoghurt or cheese) or fortified dairy alternatives. I tried to ensure my baby was meeting these requirements by serving yoghurt after dinner in the evenings or cheese as a snack, then breastfeeding on demand at home. Although milk is a great source of nutrients, it is not actually compulsory for your baby to drink it past 12 months, especially if you are still breastfeeding, as long as you ensure they are obtaining those same nutrients we discussed in Chapter 1 (pages 122–139), such as calcium, iodine and B vitamins, from other foods.

Milk amounts can often be confusing, but I hope this reassures you that when your baby is refusing milk in other environments as they transition, they are still able to get the nutrition they need in other ways after 12 months.

GETTING STARTED

Food Safety and Storage

Babies and young children are particularly vulnerable to bacteria that can cause food poisoning. Below are a few baby safety rules which I follow to reduce the risk of harmful bacteria when storing and cooking food. It is especially handy if you are batch cooking and unsure of how to cool, defrost and reheat food safely.

Preparing and serving food

- Ensure utensils are washed in hot, soapy water (remember, sterilisation is not needed from the age of six months) and keep chopping boards and surfaces clean.

- Keep pets away from any surfaces where food is prepared or eaten.

- Always wash your hands thoroughly before preparing food and after handling any raw meat, fish, egg or raw vegetables.

- Check your child's hands are clean before eating, especially if they have been touching pets or communal toys.

- Wash fruits and vegetables, and peel them if necessary, before serving them to your baby.

- Only use hen's eggs which are stamped with the British Lion or produced under the 'laid in Britain' scheme as they are less likely to cause salmonella if eaten raw or lightly cooked.

- Only serve meat, fish or shellfish that has been thoroughly cooked.

Storing food

- Allow food to cool down, ideally within one to two hours, and then store in the fridge or freezer. Food kept in the fridge should be eaten within two days. An exception to this is rice which should be cooled as quickly as possible (ideally within one hour) before storing in the fridge or freezer. Refrigerated rice should be eaten within 24 hours and should never be reheated more than once.

- Keep raw meat, fish and eggs in clean, sealed containers at the bottom of the fridge to prevent any drips falling on to other foods.

- When marinating meat, ensure this is kept in the fridge to reduce the risk of bacteria multiplying. If you are using the marinade as a sauce, ensure you have boiled it to kill any harmful bacteria before serving.

- Don't store half-eaten food as bacteria can grow if stored and reheated again.

Defrosting and reheating

- Make sure food is thoroughly defrosted before reheating it. The best way to do this is in the fridge overnight (not at room temperature) or using the microwave's defrost setting. Food that has been defrosted should be eaten within 24 hours.

- Make sure food is piping hot right the way through when reheating. Ensure it has cooled down before giving it to your baby.

- Using a microwave to reheat can lead to hot-air pockets within the food so it's important to give it a good stir while warming to make sure the heat has been evenly distributed.

- Any food that has already been cooked should only be reheated once when feeding your baby.

Food on-the-go

- Food can be made beforehand and given to baby when out and about for convenience. It can be kept in an airtight container.

- Any cold food should be eaten within four hours if stored at room temperature. It will last longer if you use a cool bag with ice packs to keep it chilled until you are ready to eat.

- Do not store the leftovers or reheat them again.

- It is easy to become distracted when out and about, so carefully supervise your baby to observe that they are swallowing food safely.

Maintaining hygiene with cups

- The corners of spouts and valves of cups can harbour bacteria. Clean them as thoroughly as possible to avoid mould or a build-up of residue.

- You can use little bottle brushes to help get into the small areas/straws or you can use a dishwasher (provided the cup is dishwasher safe).

Quick cooling

If you need to cool food down quickly, place it in an airtight container and run cold water over it or pop the container in an ice water bath. Keep stirring so it cools throughout.

Handling Setbacks

Weaning your baby is often not a straight line and there will be lots of things that crop up along the way, such as teething or illness, which can feel like one step forwards, two steps back.

Below I have discussed some of the most common weaning worries that I have seen in practice to help support you if you or your baby are experiencing them.

Teething

Teething is a normal part of your baby's development and often starts between six and twelve months (or even earlier in some cases). It can impact your weaning journey throughout and even contribute to a fussy eating phase in toddlerhood (hello molars!). Your baby's appetite can be reduced due to sore and inflamed gums and general discomfort and pain. They may be more irritable than usual and, if pain is disrupting sleep, they may also be more tired at mealtimes. If they are dribbling a lot, they may develop a 'teething rash', commonly around their mouth or chin area, so it's handy to use a bib to keep this area dry. You can use paracetamol to help relieve pain if your baby is very unsettled. If administering pain relief, try to allow 30 minutes for it to take effect before offering a meal to your baby.

As your little one may seem fussier when teething, it is really hard to know what sort of food they may be in the mood for. I have compiled a list of foods that I tend to offer at mealtimes during these challenging times and continue to use this logic even with toddlers to encourage solid intake.

A FAVOURITE FOOD:	This could be anything that generates enthusiasm for the meal, so your baby feels easily motivated to eat and may act as a distraction from the pain. This has always been grated cheese with my firstborn.
A SOFT FOOD:	Any puréed meal, rice or mashed potato – essentially anything that will reduce the effort of chewing. This will minimise the amount of work your baby's gums need to do and may make it easier for them to engage in mealtimes.
A COOLING FOOD:	Plain natural yoghurt on its own or mashed with fruit tends to be a winner, or overripe watermelon works well with my second born. It may help to soothe and cool

your little one's gums. Home-made breast milk or fruit lollies are also great, but leave them out to soften for a few minutes beforehand. (Don't offer ice cubes as they are a choking hazard.)

A HARD FOOD: Bread crusts and even raw carrot batons (if baby has no teeth to tear pieces off as they are a choking hazard) tend to be our go-to for the counter pressure on those painful gums. If your baby is older (over ten months), I tend to opt for breadsticks. This can sometimes help to relieve your baby's discomfort for a few minutes in the same way a teether or chewing on a cold metal spoon can.

You can experiment and see which foods are most comfortable for your little one when they are teething.

Although it can feel like teething goes on forever, remember it is fleeting and it will pass! Your baby's appetite should return to normal, and you can quickly get back to offering the variety of food that you were previously. Your baby may even eat more to catch up if they've had a period of food refusal.

Illness

It is common for your baby to refuse solids and only want milk feeds when they are unwell as it is an easy source of energy and nutrients. Don't worry if this happens for a few days – your baby will still remember how to eat and their appetite will return when they are feeling better, though it can take a couple of weeks to get back to normal. My firstborn caught norovirus three weeks into weaning and I felt so disappointed after getting so far, but I wish I could have told myself, 'It's OK, he will quickly pick it back up once he is better', and he did. I always suggest continuing to offer solids at the usual time of day (unless they are very distressed) so your baby stays in their routine for when they are feeling better, and they may surprise you as some babies will still want to eat even when they are ill! Whether your child is suffering from diarrhoea, vomiting, a flu-like illness or a simple cold, what I often tell parents in my clinic is that hydration is the most important thing to focus on during these times. Loss of appetite is bound to happen, but keeping an eye on how much urine your little one is producing is a helpful way of knowing how hydrated and/or poorly your baby is. Milk, soups, cereals and hydrating fruits or veggies are all good options for keeping your baby hydrated, and they may prefer to stick to a light diet for a few days, just as adults would when unwell. Following a period of illness, which may result in some weight loss, you can always offer your little one higher calorie food (see page 107) on recovery to help to regain this. It is always worth seeking advice from your family doctor if you are unsure or worried either during or after the illness.

Slow to wean

Some babies take to weaning very easily and are desperate to explore new foods and textures, gobbling it all up. However, for many, starting solids can be a slow and demanding process which requires a lot of patience from caregivers. Babies are learning a whole new world of solid food and have only ever been familiar with drinking milk. Many babies will develop these skills at their own pace, just like any other milestone, such as walking or talking. It is completely normal for them to reject and throw finger food. You may find around the nine-month mark that it all clicks and your baby develops a sudden enthusiasm for solids and consumption goes up.

Try not worry about about how much your baby is eating at one particular meal. It can be more helpful to think about what they eat over a week. The aim is to have them eating some foods from all three of the groups discussed on page 29, as well as dairy or fortified dairy alternatives if they are not drinking much milk. If your child is active and alert, has regular dirty nappies, seems generally well in themselves *and* is gaining weight, it is likely they are having enough intake. Remember, the amount of food your baby eats is not a reflection of you or your parenting skills!

If your little one seems 'slow to wean', see my top ten tips for creating a positive mealtime on page 90, which may help them (and you) to relax, and also to optimise their routine. If you feel you have addressed all of these and are still not making any progress after several weeks or there are specific feeding concerns, such as discomfort on eating or swallowing, growth problems or you are simply just extremely worried, please don't suffer in silence and reach out for professional help via your family doctor or health visitor. I have given some examples here of feeding challenges and when to seek support.

Sensitive gag reflex	Some babies may have a more sensitive gag reflex than others which can impact the speed of progressing through textures as they struggle to deal with lumpy foods or more challenging textures, resulting in excessive gagging and even vomiting. This can also understandably create a lot of parental anxiety during the early stages of weaning. Sometimes it is a case of giving it time and babies will naturally gag less. Offering baby 'resistive' foods such as hard crusts or mango stones may help to desensitise the reflex. Teethers may also help with this. Try to stay as calm as you can and, if you don't notice any improvement after a couple of months, you may need to seek support from the paediatric feeding team via your family doctor.
Tongue tie (ankyloglossia)	This is when the connecting skin (frenulum) between the tongue and floor of the mouth is too short causing reduced movement of the tongue, which can make it difficult for babies to breastfeed as they struggle to get a proper latch and maintain suction. Some babies may be unaffected by tongue tie, but, for others, if left untreated, it can result in delayed readiness for solid foods as babies may find it more challenging to move food around their mouth with their tongue or use their lips to chew and swallow. Not all family doctors, health visitors and midwives are trained to diagnose tongue tie, which can lead to misdiagnosis. It is best to seek support from a qualified tongue tie practitioner as soon as you notice any feeding issues after birth, or book an assessment with a specially-trained lactation consultant if breastfeeding.

Faltering growth

In the UK, this is the term used for when babies have a slower rate of weight gain than expected for their age and/or sex. It may be picked up on routine measurements from your health visitor or family doctor, or you may have concerns and ask for a height and weight check to record on the UK WHO standardised growth chart. (See page 250 for a link to a growth chart online.)

It's not so important what growth centile your child is on (naturally some babies will be smaller and that is perfectly fine), but how this growth centile is changing over time. Poor growth in infancy can be associated with various childhood disorders. Rapid changes in growth are something we would want to pick up and investigate early to optimise your child's health. To simplify what a centile is, if your baby is on the 25th centile, it means that 25 per cent of children (of the same age and sex) are below this weight or height. If your child is on the 50th centile, it means that 50 per cent of children (of the same age and sex) are below this weight or height so they are average. Often, if your baby is below the 0.4th centile (the lowest one), they will be followed up for growth measurements after birth.

The current thresholds for 'faltering growth' are:
- a fall across 1 or more weight centiles, if baby's birthweight was below the 9th centile
- a fall across 2 or more weight centiles, if baby's birthweight was between the 9th and 91st centiles
- a fall across 3 or more weight centiles, if baby's birthweight was above the 91st centile
- when baby's current weight is below the 2nd centile for age, whatever the birthweight

If there is any concern about faltering growth, your doctor will perform an assessment of your baby's development, general health and social environment. This will include some detailed questions related to their feeding and solid food intake. It may be helpful to record videos of feeding or mealtimes to ensure any physical problems while your baby is eating can be recognised by your healthcare professional. Your baby will usually be examined from top to toe and, if there are any positive findings, further investigations will be carried out, such as a urine sample to rule out infection or a blood test to rule out coeliac disease (see page 62).

There are some circumstances which may be associated with faltering growth, such as a premature baby, neurodevelopmental concerns or maternal postnatal depression/anxiety. Often, though, there is no specific cause and a whole host of different factors can be contributing to a drop in weight. In which case, keeping a food diary to record your baby's food intake (type/amount) and mealtime practices (setting/behaviours) can be useful to help to form a management plan and monitor any progress.

Your baby will be followed up at regular intervals for monitoring and a plan should be made that you feel is realistic and your healthcare professional is also happy with. You may receive advice on your baby's food choices, how to optimise energy and nutrient intake in their diet, as well as short-term dietary additions of high-energy/-calorie foods (see below).

Ideally, all of the above should include some or all members of the healthcare team, such as a consultant paediatrician, an infant feeding specialist, a paediatric dietitian, a speech and language therapist (with a special interest in feeding), a clinical psychologist and an occupational therapist.

High-calorie weaning diets

High-calorie weaning diets may be needed to promote weight gain particularly in babies with faltering growth. This should ideally be carried out under the supervision of a specialist paediatric doctor/dietitian.

When we started weaning my firstborn, his rate of growth slowed and he was monitored by the health visitor with repeated weight checks. I found the tips below particularly helpful:

1. Use breast milk or infant formula (this may be hypoallergenic if your little one has CMPA – see page 61) instead of water when adding to purées or cooking.

2. Add 1 teaspoon of unsalted butter to cooked foods or 1 teaspoon of olive oil if your baby is dairy-free.

3. Add grated/soft cheese to meals including mashed potato, pasta and vegetables (though be mindful of the salt content).

4. Add 1 teaspoon of nut butter (after introducing allergens – see page 84) to cooking or yoghurt.

5. Offer fruit with cream/full-fat yoghurt or unsweetened rice pudding for dessert.

6. If you are commencing weaning with vegetables/fruits, introduce new foods such as meat, fish, avocado and lentils as soon as you can following this.

7. Always use full-fat products such as milk, yoghurt and cheese until your child is at least two years old.

Struggling to poo (constipation)

During weaning, it is common for your baby's poo to change in colour, consistency and frequency as their digestive system adjusts to the newly introduced solid food. You may also find parts of undigested food mixed in with the poo, particularly as babies are still learning to chew. These changes within the digestive system mostly result in constipation, though diarrhoea can also occur during exposure to new foods – more so if your baby is suddenly consuming a lot of fibre, such as fruit, or there is a potential allergy (though this can also lead to constipation).

Constipation involves opening bowels less frequently than usual for your baby or them finding it difficult to pass stools. This is one of the most common digestive issues reported by parents/caregivers and a condition that is frequently managed in general practice. Constipation can also be triggered by a lack of fluid intake, a lack of fibre, illness, or your baby may simply have a natural tendency towards constipation. There is no strictly defined number of bowel motions to define constipation as there is such a wide spectrum of what may be normal for your child. The focus is that there is a change from your child's normal bowel habit.

Remember to increase your baby's fibre intake gradually as too much fibre can make their tummy feel full very quickly. It may help to soak lentils, beans or oats overnight before cooking them to make them more easily digestible if your little one is relatively new to the diet.

If your child is still constipated despite the techniques listed opposite, please speak to your family doctor who will take a detailed history and may consider prescribing laxatives if necessary. Always seek medical advice if you notice any blood in your baby's poo.

Signs of constipation

- Pooing fewer than three times a week (this is only a rough guide)

- Poo is large, hard or dry and/or may appear like pellets/rabbit droppings

- Unusually smelly wind or poo

- Straining or in pain when pooing[1]

- Poor or reduced appetite

- Abdominal pain relieved by pooing

- Abdomen (tummy) may feel more firm

- Bleeding during or after opening bowels

---

1 Straining can also be caused by a condition called infant dyschezia where babies appear red in the face on opening their bowels and may cry. However, it results in the passage of a normal, soft stool. The process is not fully understood, but is thought to be related to your baby still learning how to relax their pelvic floor muscles while opening their bowels and tends to occur up to nine months of age.

Tips to help with constipation

- ✓ Warm baths to relax the abdominal muscles

- ✓ Cycling your baby's legs like they are riding a bicycle while they are lying on their back

- ✓ Very gentle tummy massage in a clockwise motion

- ✓ Offering fresh fruits (particularly high water content fruits or 'p' fruits, such as prunes, pears and plums)

- ✓ Including wholegrain or 50:50 foods, such as bread and pasta, in your baby's diet

- ✓ Offering pulses, such as lentils and beans

- ✓ Offering water with meals (but be careful not to displace milk if your baby is six to twelve months old)

Managing Your Own Anxieties

Parental anxiety commonly occurs when we become overly worried about our child's health and well-being. Most of us will experience this at some point in our lives on a spectrum from mild to moderate, or it may become severe enough to impact our daily functioning. The stresses of parenthood coupled with sleep deprivation, hormonal changes, fluctuations in routine and managing uncertainty can all play a part in increasing anxiety.

Weaning is an exciting time in your little one's developmental journey and those funny faces pulled in response to first foods will be cherished memories. However, it can also feel overwhelming at times, particularly for first-time parents/caregivers. Anxiety can be especially heightened by uncertainty around allergies, fear of choking and the constant thought of, 'Am I doing this right?' I know these were all the things going through my mind with my firstborn when I became preoccupied with his weight and the food I was serving. This is why I feel it is so important to mention and offer advice to help manage any anxiety you may be experiencing. The cost of food, time for preparation and your own confidence in the kitchen can also contribute to stress during weaning.

So what can we do to help ourselves when we feel we are becoming consumed by anxiety? The very first step is recognition by paying attention to our thoughts and how those thoughts make us feel (the symptoms). It is only by recognising our thought patterns and the subsequent symptoms that we can actively step in and find ways to manage them before automatically turning to our compensatory behaviours.

Some common thought patterns may include:
- 'My child isn't taking to weaning so I must be doing it wrong.'
- 'What if my child chokes on solids? I can no longer offer finger foods.'
- 'I feel like a failure because I am too scared to introduce allergens.'
- 'My child's portion size is so small compared to others.'
- 'My cooking skills are rubbish.'

Some symptoms you may experience as a result:
- feeling stressed, irritable or constantly on edge
- having heart palpitations and/or feeling short of breath
- experiencing light-headedness, dizziness and sweating
- feeling of tension leading to muscle aches or headaches
- difficulty concentrating or feeling like you are not present
- difficulty sleeping, changes in appetite and motivation
- exhausted from worrying and feeling guilty

> To deal with these symptoms, you might then adopt the following compensatory behaviours:
> - avoidance of starting solids, introducing allergens or finger foods
> - withdrawal from social situations or making excuses to leave early
> - employing safety behaviours, such as always having someone with you when your baby is eating
> - constantly/excessively pulling food away from your baby and not allowing them to deal with it themselves

If any of these thoughts, feelings or behaviours resonate with you, I have included some tips below that you may find helpful:

BREAK THE CYCLE OF AVOIDANCE:

- Safety behaviours may help us to feel comfortable in the short term. However, after a while, they are likely to prolong anxiety and stress by reinforcing the perceived 'danger'. For example, if you are worried about introducing finger foods due to the fear of your baby choking, the longer you avoid that behaviour, the harder it may become to introduce finger food as you sit in your comfort zone. It is only after challenging yourself, for example, by serving a very mushy piece of finger food and having confidence that your baby was able to handle it without choking, will you disprove your thought and subsequently reduce the anxiety.

- We can also challenge these patterns of thoughts and behaviours by rationalising them with evidence. For example, you can write down, 'My child is not taking to weaning – I must be doing it wrong' and then write down next to it any facts that prove or disprove your initial thought. You will soon start to realise that there is probably very little objective evidence that what you are doing is wrong, which can help you to challenge unhelpful thoughts and regain confidence.

- Lastly, you may want to gradually expose yourself to stressful situations that you have been avoiding in a term known as 'graded exposure'. For example, if you have been avoiding eating out or in a social setting with your baby, you could start by going out to eat for 20 minutes then coming home. You can steadily increase this time by 10 minutes. It can work to gradually face any fears or phobias and is a strategy often used to manage panic attacks/anxiety.

MANAGE THE PHYSICAL SYMPTOMS:

- Our bodies tend to go into an evolutionary state of 'fight or flight' to a perceived stressor such as choking. This causes lots of the hormone adrenaline to be pumped around our bodies and takes us back to the days of being confronted by a sabre-toothed tiger, where this response may have once been helpful. In current times, repeated amounts of adrenaline is not so useful, especially over a long period of time, and can lead to many of the physical symptoms listed above, such as feeling tense and on edge. This can be controlled by deep and gentle breathing exercises, such as the 3-4-7 method where you breathe in for 3 seconds, hold your breath for 4 seconds and breathe out for 7 seconds, to help to slow down our heart rate and prevent a full-blown panic attack.

- Another useful technique to relax your body is to practise individually tensing all your muscles and relaxing them again one by one, starting with your head and neck, then moving down towards your legs and toes. This 'progressive muscle relaxation', as it is known, can be a helpful way of releasing tension physically, but also allowing you to feel lighter mentally.

- Exercise also releases endorphins or 'feel-good' transmitters into the bloodstream which is a great way to reduce stress. I know this may not be realistic while balancing childcare, but even going for a brisk walk with the pram, jumping up and down on the spot, dancing to music or doing star jumps in your lounge all count as movement and can get your heart rate up to provide some benefit.

SEEK HELP:

- Many of the tips above are self-guided. However, it can be difficult to find the motivation or clarity to follow this through when you are feeling particularly anxious or low. It is important to be open and honest with the people around you so they can understand and help with how you are feeling. Remember, anxiety is very treatable if you have the right support around you.

- Don't be afraid to reach out for professional support via your family doctor. In the UK, you can be referred for counselling or directed to self-refer, which often involves cognitive behavioural therapy and encompasses the techniques above guided by a counsellor. Your family doctor can also discuss if any medications may help physically, such as beta blockers or antidepressants. Sometimes, just talking through options and knowing support is there is enough.

I want to close this section with my favourite weaning mantras, which have really helped me during times of anxiety. I have to admit that I would often say them and not really believe them, especially at the start, but with constant repetition (a little bit like affirmations), they have really become ingrained in my mind. Now, when I have stressful moments or periods of fussy eating in toddlerhood or even when my youngest weaner is having an 'off' day, I instantly come back to these and feel so much more relaxed. You can adapt them to address your specific anxieties with your baby. As cheesy as it may sound, I think every caregiver should stick them on the wall or write them down in their notes app and remind themselves of them daily!

My weaning mantras

How much my baby eats is not a reflection of my parenting skills.

—

Exposing my baby to a new food is still a win even if they didn't eat it.

—

Not all of my cooking will be enjoyed and that's completely normal.

—

My worth as a parent/caregiver is not measured in portion size.

—

Offering an alternative on occasion doesn't make me a failure.

—

There is so much more to mealtime than just food time.

—

The table may be messy, but my baby is learning and exploring.

—

Fussy eating can be a normal part of the weaning journey.

—

Keep the table a calm and happy place for all.

I hope this chapter has helped you to feel more confident in the practical aspects of weaning, addressing mealtimes as a whole and creating an optimal environment for feeding.

Once you get through those early stages of your baby learning to eat and they have adjusted to self-feeding, you will inevitably encounter setbacks along the way, but you can always refer back to this chapter to guide you through when you are feeling unsure. I also hope it gives you a better idea of when to seek further support from a healthcare professional and the confidence to ask for help when you are worried.

In Part Two, I am super excited to share a whole host of new recipes with you that are balanced and contain the important nutrients we talked about in the last chapter, without compromising on time or flavour, which are both important to me! This means the whole family can truly enjoy one meal without grown-ups feeling like they are eating 'baby food' or worrying that food is unsafe for your baby. Weaning is a wonderful opportunity for the whole family to look at their dietary habits and make positive and sustainable changes to mealtimes. I cannot stress the importance of trying to eat together when you can, too, and ideally the same meals as your baby. You are their biggest role model – plus who has time to cook multiple meals every night?!

I sincerely hope you and your family enjoy these recipes and they help to take the pressure off weaning and meal prepping.

GETTING STARTED

Weaning principles

Below I have outlined the weaning principles which I feel are the most important to keep in mind. You can keep referring to this list at any time, especially if you feel short of time and want to remind yourself of the basics.

1. **Be patient:** babies may spend a lot of time squashing, playing with and dropping food at the start of weaning without much going in, which is all part of learning how to eat. Avoid putting pressure on them – once they are ready, the majority will start to eat more.

2. **Move gradually:** breast milk or infant formula is still an important source of nutrition and food should not be replacing milk in the early days, but simply complementing it. Transition slowly by gradually increasing the amount of solid intake to allow your baby's digestive system to get used to the new foods.

3. **Eat together:** when you can, try to eat together, even if it's just a small amount of food, as mealtimes are not just about eating but socialising too. Your baby will learn so much about how to eat from watching you and other family members.

4. **Offer iron-rich foods:** once your baby is consuming solids, try to focus on offering iron-rich foods so they can absorb all the nutrients they need to thrive. Remember, every bite counts, so opt for whole foods where you can (but don't beat yourself up when you can't).

5. **Adopt a baby-led approach:** whether you choose to start with purées, finger foods or both, take a baby-led approach by allowing your little one to be in control of putting spoons/food to their mouths (where you can) and ending the meal when they show signs of fullness.

6. **Offer a cup:** it's easy to focus so much on solids that you forget about cup drinking. Start offering an open cup from the start of weaning so your baby becomes familiar with the taste of water, sipping and swallowing, and holding a cup independently.

7. **Offer variety:** a baby can't learn to like a food they are never shown, so remember variety is key! It doesn't mean you have to go out and buy lots of different expensive foods, but change up meals with anything you have at home. It doesn't have to look like a conventional meal. Use tinned or frozen options for convenience.

8. **Introduce allergens early:** there is so much new research showing that early, frequent exposure to common allergens, such as peanut and egg, may help to reduce the risk of babies developing an allergy in later life, so try to get them in early and maintain them.

9. **Get messy:** allowing your baby to explore is great for their sensory development and becoming familiar with lots of different textures. If you are like me and find this part challenging, try to put as many provisions in place as possible to help with the cleaning up. If possible, let your partner/relative start bath time while your baby is still eating so you can pop them straight in once they're finished. I promise it gets less and less messy as time goes on!

10. **Comparison is the thief of joy:** of course, this is a natural thing that we all do to help us know if we are doing things 'right'. But remember, babies will move at their own individual pace in the same way as they do with walking or talking. They all have different energy requirements too. Don't chase perfection when it comes to starting solids – embrace your own unique journey. Weaning is by far one of the most enjoyable and rewarding parts of parenting!

PART 2

Now we have talked about the principles and practicalities of weaning, in this part I'll share with you my inspiration for creating balance in your kitchen without compromising on time and flavour. My main focus here is to simplify meals as much as possible to reduce cooking time and non-essential ingredients (because we have enough to think about already!) while keeping variety within meals. I've also added some of my favourite authentic childhood recipes for those of you looking for more wholesome and satisfying family meals.

Part Two is divided into transition meals, breakfast, lunch, dinner, puddings, and snacks and dips. Many of the recipes are interchangeable, so for example, lots of the breakfasts can be used for snacks and lunches can become dinners, and vice versa. I have also included some of my most popular and original social media favourites that have become staples in your kitchens over the years.

Many of these recipes were created from the heart and I sincerely hope they bring as much joy, fun, love and connection to your kitchen as they have to ours.

Storage advice

I receive lots of queries relating to storage advice and so I thought I would share some of my blanket rules when it comes to cooking. Most of the recipes can be safely stored in an airtight container in the fridge for approximately two days, and one month in the freezer, to maintain the best quality. Some foods can be stored in the freezer for longer, but this depends on the type of food. For example, cooked stews, lentils or soups containing meat or vegetables may last for up to two to three months.

Don't forget to carefully package your food, separate it into smaller portions if needed and label the packages with the current date to ensure you don't lose track of how long the food has been kept.

Specific ingredients

There are certain ingredients used in the recipes that can vary in terms of texture or flavour. For example, peanut butter can be smooth or crunchy and yoghurt can be plain or sweetened, so you may be wondering which type to use. I therefore thought it would be a good idea to mention the safest or ideal way to offer these ingredients to your baby in one place. I hope this list makes things easier to navigate:

- **Peanut butter:** smooth, salt-free, palm oil-free.
- **Yoghurt:** natural, unsweetened, full-fat.
- **Butter:** unsalted, if possible.
- **Plant-based milk:** see the box on page 43.
- **Dairy and spreads:** ideally full-fat (see page 30).
- **Paprika:** sweet is often used in the recipes.
- **Potatoes:** floury potatoes are usually best.
- **Tuna:** in water, if possible.

Herbs and spices

When it comes to creating flavour, there are so many ways to do this without the addition of salt. Simply mixing together different blends of herbs and spices or adding citrus fruits such as lemon can go a long way. My advice is to invest in herbs and spices at the start of weaning as once then they are in the cupboard, they are there for any last-minute cooking. You can also freeze fresh herbs such as parsley or coriander and then throw them straight into cooking to avoid food waste. You will find that many of the spices are optional depending on your family's preference – some people love oodles of flavour, while others prefer to just use a smidge. These recipes are flexible, and you can start with less and build it up over time. You can also add salt or chilli flakes to grown-up portions at the end, which my husband and I sometimes do for an extra kick.

Alternative Foods for Allergens

One of the most common questions I am asked when sharing recipes is 'What alternatives can I use?' for those who have allergies but still want to enjoy the recipe. There are some great substitutes depending on the recipe itself. I have noted down a few common swaps, but they may not work in every recipe. For example, some alternatives to egg, such as banana and apple purée, will work well as binding agents. However, egg substitutions don't tend to work well in recipes where three or more eggs are used.

Common allergen	Alternative
1 EGG (IN BAKING)	Chia egg: 1 tsp chia seeds + 3 tbsp water Flax egg: 1 tsp flax seeds + 3 tbsp water ½ ripe banana ¼ cup apple purée ¼ cup puréed avocado
SCRAMBLED EGG	Scrambled tofu
PEANUT BUTTER	Almond nut butter (1:1) Cashew nut butter (1:1) Sunflower seed butter (nut free) (1:1)
CHEESE	Vegan cheese*, nutritional yeast*
YOGHURT	Soy yoghurt (fortified) or any plant-based yoghurt (1:1)
COW'S MILK	Soy milk (fortified) or any plant-based milk (1:1)
BUTTER	Milk-free margarine (1:1) Olive oil (3:4)
WHEAT/WHEAT FLOUR	Oat or almond flour (baking) Chickpea flour (fritters) Quinoa Cornstarch to thicken sauces (2:1)
SESAME HUMMUS (TAHINI)	Smashed peas (see recipe page 243)

* Many vegan cheeses are not fortified so will not have the same nutritional value as dairy cheese.

Transition Meals

CHAPTER 3

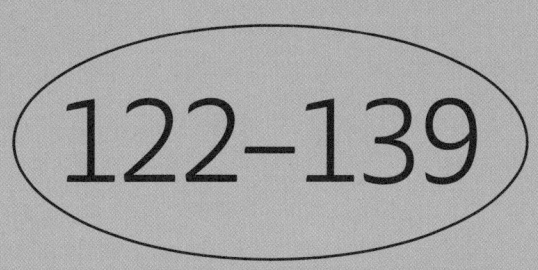

Once you have introduced your baby to their first tastes, you might be left wondering what to do next. It takes time for you and your baby to build confidence around mealtimes and you might be feeling a little lost when it comes to progressing from single veggies to full-blown meals – I know I certainly felt this way with my firstborn.

Some families will feel comfortable heading straight to giving their baby what they are eating which is great; however, I have created some transition meals to gently guide you towards offering more balanced meals with soft squishable foods if you are feeling at a loose end. All the transition recipes are simple to make, iron-rich and can still be enjoyed by the whole family to avoid having to cook twice. You can, of course, continue to keep any favourites in your family's diet long after weaning.

TRANSITION MEALS

6+ MONTHS

Spiced Orange Porridge

This simple, warming dish is ideal when you can't be bothered to cook and still want to give your baby something nutritious. What I love about porridge is the ability to easily vary the ingredients and texture to suit your baby. This particular recipe packs in extra nutrients and has a deep-spiced citrussy flavour that really warms the senses.

PREP: 5 minutes
COOK: 2 minutes

SERVES: 1 PERSON (BABY PORTION)

- 15g rolled oats (or fortified instant oats such as Ready Brek)
- 200ml milk of choice
- ⅓ carrot, finely grated
- 1 tsp smooth peanut butter
- pinch of ground cinnamon
- a little grated orange zest

Put all the ingredients in a microwaveable bowl and simply microwave for 30 seconds, stir, then microwave again for another 30 seconds (you can cook it in a pan on the hob if you prefer).

If the texture is a bit gooey or dry, just stir in another splash of milk – this will also help to cool it down before serving.

Tip
Use this as a base and alter ingredients daily by changing the fruit or veg, nut butter or seeds to help expose your baby to different flavours. Try to serve the same fruit in the porridge as a finger food to help familiarise your baby with the natural colour, texture, taste and smell of the fruit.

6+ MONTHS

Mini Avo-banana Pancakes

Finger food doesn't have to be fussy – these nutritious four-ingredient pancakes are made largely from household cupboard staples. The avocado gives them a super-soft texture, which makes them ideal for early weaning.

PREP: 5 minutes
COOK: 5–10 minutes

MAKES: 10–12 SMALL PANCAKES

- ½ ripe avocado, stoned and peeled
- ½ ripe banana, peeled
- 1 egg
- 3 tbsp rolled oats (or instant oats)
- olive oil, for frying

Mash the avocado and banana together in a bowl with a fork until smooth. Crack in the egg, then add the oats and stir to combine.

Heat a little olive oil in a frying pan over a medium-high heat, add single tablespoons of the mixture to the pan, cook for 2½ minutes, then flip and continue to cook until fully cooked on both sides. Remove from the pan and repeat with the rest of the mixture.

Leave to cool for a few minutes then serve them whole or halved, to make it easy for your baby to grab hold of them.

Tip
This works without the avocado if you use a whole banana and you can add any other fruit such as raspberries or strawberries.

Simple Salmon, Broccoli and Potato

6+ MONTHS

If you have followed me on Instagram for a while, you will know that this simple dish is one of my favourite classic dinners and I have always found it instantly comforting! So I had to create a version that I can still eat with my babies. This is one of our regular weeknight meals.

PREP: 15–20 minutes
COOK: 20 minutes

SERVES: 2 ADULTS AND 2 CHILDREN

- 300g floury potatoes, peeled
- 2 skinless salmon fillets (about 220–250g each)
- 4 tbsp lemon juice
- a little fresh parsley, finely chopped
- olive oil, for drizzling
- 2 tsp dried mixed herbs or thyme
- 1 medium head of broccoli, roughly chopped into florets

Stab the potatoes with a fork and cook in boiling water for 15–20 minutes until softened.

Preheat the oven to 200°C and line a baking tray with foil.

Put the salmon fillets on the lined tray and drizzle 2 tablespoons of lemon juice over each fillet. Sprinkle with some parsley and bake in the oven for 20 minutes until cooked through.

Drain the potatoes then put them on a separate foil-lined baking tray and drizzle them with a generous amount of olive oil. Sprinkle them with the mixed herbs or thyme and roast the potatoes in the oven for 20 minutes at the same time as the salmon.

While the potatoes and salmon are in the oven, steam or boil the broccoli until soft (leaving the florets in their cooking water after cooking will keep them soft and juicy).

Serve to your baby either as finger food with flaked pieces of salmon, batons of potato and whole broccoli florets, or mash it all together and pre-load it onto a spoon, or do both!

Tip
I love to roast potatoes for longer, until crispy, for myself and I will often stir-fry the broccoli in some olive oil and garlic after boiling, for extra flavour.

6+ MONTHS

Four-veg Frittata

Packed with veggies, this frittata makes a great soft finger food for early weaning and it is made in one dish, which saves on washing up. I love to snack on this too, as it keeps me feeling full throughout the day.

PREP: 5 minutes
COOK: 30 minutes

SERVES: 2 ADULTS AND 2 CHILDREN

- ½ courgette, grated
- 1 carrot, peeled and finely grated
- handful of spinach, finely chopped
- 3 or 4 broccoli florets, steamed or boiled (optional if time to pre-cook)
- 6 eggs
- 1 tsp dried mixed herbs
- ½ tsp freshly ground black pepper
- 40g cheddar cheese, grated (optional)

Preheat the oven to 180°C.

Grease a roughly 21cm ovenproof dish with butter or oil. Squeeze out any excess water after grating the vegetables with a tea towel and chop the cooked broccoli into smaller pieces. Place the grated courgette, grated carrot, chopped spinach and cooked broccoli into the ovenproof dish.

In a separate bowl, whisk the eggs, mixed herbs and black pepper then pour the mixture over the veggies into the ovenproof dish. Sprinkle the cheese evenly on top (if using) and bake for 30 minutes, until cooked through.

Leave to cool before slicing into strips.

Tip
The frittata strips are easier to hold with little hands when fully cooled as the texture will be a little firmer. Serve with a side of steamed peppers (skin removed) to increase the vitamin C content of the meal.

6+ MONTHS

Grandma's Feel-good Lentil Rice

KITCHERI

This Indian-inspired dish has long been made during times of illness and is believed, in the Ayurvedic medicine tradition, to help remove toxins and aid digestion. Growing up, if we were ever poorly, it was my mother's go-to recipe and is now mine for my babies. The spices are optional and offer a warm, earthy flavour.

PREP: 5 minutes
COOK: 35 minutes

SERVES: 2 ADULTS AND 2 CHILDREN (GENEROUSLY)

- 150g basmati rice
- 150g yellow lentils
- knob of butter or 3–4 tbsp olive oil
- 3 garlic cloves, finely chopped
- 2cm piece of ginger, peeled and grated
- 1 tsp cumin seeds or ground cumin
- 3 whole cloves or ¼ tsp ground cloves (optional)
- 2cm piece of cinnamon stick (optional)
- 1 litre water
- ½ tsp turmeric
- ½ tsp garam masala
- ½ tsp freshly ground black pepper
- handful of fresh coriander, finely chopped, to serve (optional)

Put the rice and lentils in a sieve together and rinse under cold running water until the water runs clear.

Heat the butter or oil in a saucepan over a medium heat then add the garlic, ginger and cumin (and cinnamon stick and cloves, if using) and cook for 30–60 seconds until fragrant. When the cumin seeds start to sizzle, add the drained rice and lentils, the water and the remaining spices. Bring to the boil and cook for 5 minutes then reduce the heat to low, cover and cook for 25–30 minutes, stirring occasionally to ensure the rice and lentils don't stick to bottom of pan, adding more water if you want the dish to have a looser, soupier consistency.

Turn off the heat, remove the lid, cover the pan with a tea towel, replace the lid and leave to stand for 10 minutes before serving. Remove the cloves and cinnamon stick, if using, before serving (due to choking risk).

Tip
You can add fish for protein or frozen veggies for extra goodness. It is lovely served with some cooling natural yoghurt.

6+ MONTHS

Spiced Vegetables

PAV BHAJI

Originating from the streets of Mumbai, this mildly spiced vegetable curry (bhaji) is traditionally served in buns (pav). It's perfect for introducing your baby to a variety of flavours and can be prepared as a purée or served as a thicker texture. The beauty of home cooking is being able to adjust the spices to your family's taste – you can start off mild and increase the quantities a little each time you make it.

PREP: 15 minutes
COOK: 45 minutes

SERVES: 2 ADULTS AND 2 CHILDREN (GENEROUSLY)

- 450g floury potatoes, peeled and cut into chunks
- 1 cauliflower head, cut into florets
- 100g frozen peas
- 1 carrot, peeled and roughly chopped
- 500ml water
- 1 white onion, diced
- 4 garlic cloves, crushed
- 2cm piece of ginger, peeled and grated
- 400g tin chopped tomatoes
- 2 tbsp olive oil or unsalted butter

OPTIONAL SPICES
- 1 tsp ground coriander
- 1 tsp ground cumin
- 2 tsp garam masala
- ½ tsp turmeric

TO SERVE
- fresh coriander, chopped

Cook all the vegetables (excluding the onion and tomatoes) in a large saucepan with the 500ml water for 25–30 minutes, adding more water if it starts to look dry. Drain any cooking water from the pan and place the water to one side for later, and mash the vegetables.

In a separate large, deep frying pan, fry the onion in butter or olive oil over a medium heat for 5–7 minutes until it starts to become translucent. Add the garlic and ginger and fry for 2 minutes until fragrant, then add the chopped tomatoes and cook for 5 minutes until the tomatoes are mashable and the sauce starts to thicken. Add all the spices (if using) and cook for 15–30 seconds until fragrant.

Add the mashed vegetables to the pan with 100–150ml of the reserved vegetable cooking water to soften the mixture. Cook for about 10 minutes until it thickens to the desired consistency, mashing the vegetables further while cooking, if needed. Remove from the heat and stir in the fresh coriander.

Serve with warm buttered toast or buns for older ones. Blend if desired for babies.

6+ MONTHS

Smashed Tuna Jackets

You may find yourself wondering how to serve your own 'go-to' meals to a baby, so this one has been adapted to suit them while still being able to enjoy yours. All you have to do is scoop out the potato, mash it with the chosen filling then pop it back in the potato skin for your baby to eat with a spoon – easy peasy!

PREP: 5 minutes
COOK: 10 minutes (longer if you want to crisp it in the oven)

SERVES: 1 ADULT AND 1 CHILD

- 1 jacket potato, washed
- olive oil, for brushing (optional)
- 1 tbsp full-fat unsweetened Greek yoghurt
- 2 tbsp tinned tuna (in water, not brine)
- 1 tbsp grated cheddar cheese (optional)
- 1 tbsp unsalted butter
- 1 tsp finely chopped fresh parsley
- lemon juice, to taste

Prick the potato a few times with a fork, place on a microwavable plate and cook in the microwave on high for 7–10 minutes until soft (how long it takes will depend on the size of the potato and the power of the microwave), or bake it in a hot oven until cooked through.

Once cooked, if you have time, brush it with some olive oil and place in an oven heated to 150°C for 15–20 minutes to allow the skin to crisp up. If you are short on time, skip this step.

Cut the potato in half as soon as it's cool enough to handle and scoop out the potato. Retain the skin.

In a bowl, mix the potato with the yoghurt, tuna, grated cheese (if using), butter and parsley and add a squeeze of lemon juice. The cheese should naturally melt when it combines with the potato. Place the potato mix back into the potato skins and allow your baby to get stuck in!

Tip
Add a splash of cold milk (of choice) to the potato mix to adjust the consistency and cool the dish down quicker, if needed.

TRANSITION MEALS

6+ MONTHS

Sweet Potato and Black Bean Mash

This combination works so well, and it's a nutritional powerhouse for your baby. The vitamin C in the sweet potato helps your body to absorb the iron from the black beans. It also makes a great side for a Mexican night! In the early days of weaning, you may wish to just cook the sweet potato and black beans, then slowly build more flavour and texture with the full recipe.

PREP: 5 minutes
COOK: 10 minutes

SERVES: 2 PEOPLE

- 1 sweet potato
- olive oil, for frying
- 115g tinned black beans, drained and rinsed

OPTIONAL
(LONGER VERSION)
- ½ onion, finely chopped
- 1 garlic clove, crushed or finely chopped
- ½ tsp ground cumin
- ¼ tsp paprika
- ¼ tsp dried oregano
- 1 fresh plum tomato

Prick the sweet potato a few times with a fork, place on a microwavable plate and cook in the microwave for approximately 10 minutes until soft (how long it takes will depend on the size of the potato and the power of the microwave), or bake it in a hot oven until cooked through, then peel off the skin and mash.

Heat a drizzle of olive oil in a frying pan over a medium heat and skip to the next step for the simple recipe. If you want to add more flavour, fry the onion, garlic, spices and oregano in the pan for 5 minutes until translucent then add the tomato and fry for another 5 minutes until softened, then squish the tomato with the back of a spoon. Tip in the black beans and warm through for a couple of minutes.

Mix the black beans into the sweet potato mash, ensuring the beans are squished before serving to your baby to avoid them being a choking risk.

Tip
See my quesadilla recipe on page 178 for how to level this up to a family meal.

6+ MONTHS

Shredded Chicken and Avocado Fusilli

This recipe was created on a day where I had to work with whatever was in the fridge. The first time I served it, my baby was skeptical but has devoured it ever since. Avocado is a source of healthy fats and can be quickly turned into a sauce, all while the pasta is cooking. Introducing your baby to meat can be daunting – however, finely shredding it into the pasta for some iron-rich protein can be a good start.

PREP: 5 minutes
COOK: 10 minutes

SERVES: 2 ADULTS AND 2 CHILDREN (GENEROUSLY)

- 200g fusilli pasta
- 1 ripe avocado, halved, stoned and peeled
- juice of ½ lemon
- handful of fresh basil
- 1 cooked skinless, boneless chicken breast (or leftover cooked chicken)

Cook the pasta in boiling water according to the packet instructions.

While the pasta is cooking, put the avocado, lemon juice and basil in a blender and blend until smooth. Add a splash of pasta cooking water and blend again to make a thinner sauce. Drain the pasta and mix it with the sauce.

Finely shred the chicken with your fingers (use scissors to chop long pieces smaller if needed) and stir it into the pasta.

Serve the pasta and chicken as finger food to your baby. Add salt and chilli flakes for grown-ups!

Tip
You may want to overcook the pasta for a few minutes until very soft, to make it easier for your baby to chew and swallow. Fusilli tends to be good for little hands to grip.

TRANSITION MEALS

6+ MONTHS

Broccoli Omelette Strips

I find omelettes are a fantastic way to include those veggies from first tastes and repeat their exposure to your baby in a very simple and achievable recipe. Your baby may be taking to finger food or want more control, so these strips are great for practising self-feeding.

PREP: 5 minutes
COOK: 5 minutes

SERVES: 1 ADULT AND 1 CHILD

- 1 egg
- 2–3 raw small broccoli florets, diced into small pieces and stems removed
- olive oil, for frying

Crack the egg into a bowl and whisk with a fork, then add the broccoli and mix thoroughly.

Heat a drizzle of olive oil in a frying pan over a medium heat, pour in the egg and broccoli mix and cook for 5 minutes, flipping it over when the base is cooked, to ensure both sides are fully cooked.

Remove from the pan and cut into strips to serve to baby.

Tip
You can use any veggies for this recipe, such as grated courgette, carrot or chopped spinach. Leftover cooked veggies from the night before work too. It is a quicker version of frittata but creates a different texture.

Breakfast

CHAPTER 4

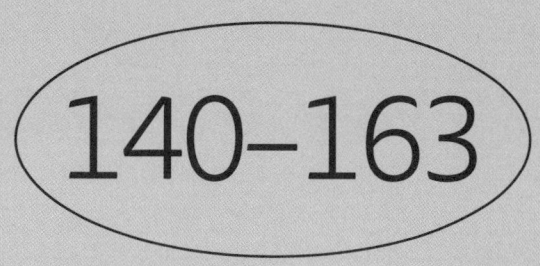

It can be really easy to get stuck in a rut with breakfast in terms of serving the same cereal or porridge that you know your baby loves, especially when you are rushing out of the door or focusing more on lunch and dinner options. I have therefore tried to create some simple yet varied breakfasts to break things up a little and allow your baby to try new flavours.

You can experiment with these recipes on the weekends and incorporate the ones you love into your weekly schedule. There are also lots of on-the-go options which can be made the night before and batch cooked for the week ahead, such as muffins, scones, crêpes or breads – so handy if you are also doing the school run. These recipes can double-up as a snack for later on in the day or to enjoy during a parent and baby playdate.

7+ MONTHS

Loaded Toast – Three Ways

This is for the mornings when you have been up all night, you don't want to add to the mental load and just need a breakfast you can whip up in five minutes – trust me, we have had many nights like this. Just think about what extras you have in the fridge that you can pop onto the toast for more nutrients and exposure to new flavours for your little one, such as hummus, cream cheese, avocado or tinned fish.

---

one

Avocado and Egg Loaded Toast

PREP: 5 minutes
COOK: 5 minutes

SERVES: 1 BABY (WITH SOME LEFTOVERS)

- olive oil, for drizzling
- slice of bread, toasted and buttered

Heat a little olive oil in a frying pan over a medium heat, add the egg and scramble until fully cooked.

Mash the avocado flesh in a bowl then add the scrambled egg and mix until it is all mashed together.

Spread onto buttered toast and slice into long fingers to make it easy for your baby to hold.

two

Yoghurt and Raspberry Chia Jam Loaded Toast

PREP: 5 minutes

SERVES: 1 BABY (WITH SOME LEFTOVERS)

- 1½ tbsp full-fat unsweetened Greek yoghurt
- 1 tbsp Raspberry Chia Jam (page 245)
- slice of bread, toasted and buttered

Mix together the yoghurt and jam, then spread onto buttered toast and slice into long fingers.

Tip
Try with blueberry or strawberry chia jam – see page 245.

three

Cream Cheese and Grated Cucumber Loaded Toast

PREP: 5 minutes

SERVES: 1 BABY (WITH SOME LEFTOVERS)

- 1½ tbsp cream cheese
- slice of bread, toasted
- 1½ tbsp grated cucumber

Spread the cream cheese on the toast. Add the grated cucumber on top and slice into long fingers.

BREAKFAST

6+ MONTHS

Nutty Overnight Raspberry Oats

Because who doesn't love it when breakfast is already made and all you have to do is whip it out of the fridge and add fresh fruit. The optional chia seeds are an excellent source of fibre, heart-healthy fats and minerals. Just ensure they have been soaked beforehand.

PREP: 5 minutes
COOK: 5 minutes

SERVES: 1 PERSON (BABY PORTION)

- 1 tbsp full-fat unsweetened Greek yoghurt
- 1 tsp smooth nut butter of choice
- splash of milk of choice
- ½ tsp chia seeds (optional)
- 20g rolled oats
- handful of fresh raspberries

Combine the Greek yoghurt, nut butter and milk in a bowl, then add the chia seeds (if using) and mix again. Add the oats and another splash of milk and mix until combined. Add further splashes of milk until the mix has a loose consistency. Cover and leave in the fridge overnight.

The next morning, heat the raspberries in a microwavable bowl in the microwave for 20–30 seconds until they are starting to break down, then mash further and add to your chilled overnight oats.

Tip
Alternate the fruit according to what is in season – this recipe works with blueberries, strawberries or raspberries, or grated ripe apple or pear.

BREAKFAST

7+ MONTHS

Mini Lentil Crêpes

If you are looking for a vegan breakfast option that doesn't compromise on time or flavour, then this is for you. The crispy edges of these savoury crêpes make them perfect for babies to hold and chew on. They are thin too, so will melt in their mouth. They also make a very portable, mess-free nutritious snack.

PREP: 5 minutes
COOK: 10 minutes

MAKES: 8 CRÊPES

- 80g red lentils, soaked and drained if you have time (see Tips below)
- 1cm piece of ginger
- small handful of fresh coriander
- ½ tsp ground cumin
- 150ml water
- olive oil, for frying
- Tomato Raita (page 237), to serve

Put all the ingredients (except the oil) in a blender and blend until completely smooth and all lentils have been broken down.

Heat a generous amount of olive oil in a frying pan over a high heat and wait until the pan/oil are piping hot. Give the mixture a stir, then pour an eighth (approx. 2 tbsp) into the centre of the pan and use the back of a spoon to gently spread it around in a circular motion to make a thin pancake. Fry for 2–3 minutes, until the mixture has cooked and set, then flip and do the same on the other side.

Remove the crêpe from the pan and repeat with the remaining batter. Leave to cool down for a couple of minutes and serve with Tomato Raita (the vitamin C will help the body absorb the iron from the lentils).

Tips

Soaking the lentils in water for a few hours will make them easier to digest but is not a necessity. Add fresh chopped green chillies for grown-ups, sprinkling them on top while the pancakes cook – my husband and I love this!

BREAKFAST

7+ MONTHS

Fruity Muffins

A light and fluffy muffin with extra protein from the yoghurt that can be topped with any berries you have to hand. Plain flour can also be used instead of oat flour for an even softer texture. It also works well as an on-the-go, filling snack, so I always sneak a couple in my lunch bag for work!

PREP: 5 minutes
COOK: 15–20 minutes

MAKES: 12 SMALL MUFFINS

- 150g oats (rolled oats or instant oats)
- 200g full-fat unsweetened Greek yoghurt
- 2 ripe bananas, peeled
- 2 eggs
- 1 tsp baking powder

OPTIONAL TOPPINGS
- strawberries, quartered
- blueberries, squished
- raspberries, halved

Preheat the oven to 200°C and grease a 12-hole cupcake tin with butter or oil.

Put the oats in a blender and blend to a flour for 1 minute, then add the remaining ingredients and blend just until smooth. Avoid over-blending, as it may make the muffins denser after cooking.

Divide the mixture evenly among the 12 cupcake holes and add your choice of fruit toppings (about 3 berries per muffin).

Bake in the oven for 15–20 minutes until golden brown.

Remove from the oven and leave to cool for at least 10 minutes in the tin before removing them (to help them keep their shape).

Tip
You can add chocolate chips with the fruit toppings for older children.

BREAKFAST

7+ MONTHS

Green Masala Omelette

Stimulate your baby's senses with this green omelette, which packs in spinach and plenty of flavour, and can be finished off with a comforting cheesy topping.

PREP: 5 minutes
COOK: 10 minutes

SERVES: 1-2 PEOPLE

- 2 eggs
- 2 handfuls of spinach
- small handful of fresh, finely chopped coriander
- ¼ tsp garam masala
- ¼ tsp chilli powder (optional)
- ½ tsp black pepper (optional)
- ½ tsp ground cumin (optional)
- ½ chopped onion or tomato (optional)
- olive oil, for drizzling
- 15g cheddar cheese, grated (optional)

Put the eggs, spinach and coriander in a blender and blend until smooth.

Heat a splash of olive oil in a frying pan over a medium-high heat. Once hot, fry the onion/tomato (if using) until sauteed then pour the egg mixture in and spread it around the pan evenly. Cook on one side for a minute or two, then flip and sprinkle with the cheese (if using).

Remove from the pan once the egg's cooked and cut into strips for easy finger-food, or squares if your baby is 9m+ and has found their pincer grasp.

Tip
You can turn this mix into individual muffins: finely chop the spinach and coriander and sprinkle them evenly among 8 holes of a greased muffin tin. Beat the eggs with the spices (and onion/tomato if using) then pour the batter evenly over the spinach and coriander. Sprinkle with cheese (if using) and cook in the oven at 200°C for 15 minutes to create masala egg muffins.

7+ MONTHS

My Original Weetabix Muffins

This recipe was a huge hit on my social media channels. I created it as a way to make an iron-rich baby breakfast without having to wipe the Weetabix 'cement' off the highchair – busy parents simply don't have time for endless cleaning first thing in the morning.

PREP: 10 minutes
COOK: 25–30 minutes

MAKES: 6 MUFFINS (OR 12 MINI MUFFINS)

- 1 ripe banana, peeled
- 3 Weetabix (or any wheat biscuits), crushed with a rolling pin or your hands
- 1 egg, beaten
- 85g plain flour
- 150ml milk of choice
- 1 tsp baking powder
- 75g raspberries (or soft berries of choice)

Preheat the oven to 180°C and generously grease 6 holes of a muffin tin with butter or olive oil.

Mash the banana in a bowl until smooth. Add the egg and milk then whisk to combine. Add the crushed Weetabix, flour and baking powder and mix until well combined. Fold in the raspberries or fruit of choice, then evenly distribute the batter among the 6 muffin holes. Bake in the oven for 25–30 minutes, or until golden brown.

Remove from the oven and leave to cool in the tin.

Tip
These are great for batch cooking and defrosting if you need something quick on the school run.

BREAKFAST

7+ MONTHS

Rise and Shine Loaf

A simple, refined-sugar-free bake that's ideal for an on-the-go breakfast. It is packed with protein, fibre and natural sugars from the fruit to set you and your baby up for the day. It even sneaks in some veggies!

PREP: 10 minutes
COOK: 25–30 minutes

MAKES: ABOUT 10 SLICES

- 90g rolled oats
- 1 large ripe banana, peeled
- 2 eggs
- 65g unsalted butter, softened
- 1 apple, peeled and grated
- 1 carrot, grated
- 90g plain flour
- 1 tsp baking powder
- ½ tsp ground cinnamon

Preheat the oven to 180°C and grease a 900g (2lb) loaf tin with butter or oil, or line it with baking parchment.

Put the oats in a blender and blend to make oat flour.

Mash the banana in a bowl then add all the wet ingredients and mix to combine: the eggs, butter, apple and carrot. In a separate bowl, mix the dry ingredients: the oat flour, plain flour, baking powder and cinnamon. Add the dry ingredients to the wet and mix well, then pour the mixture into the prepared tin, level it out and bake for 25–30 minutes.

Check the loaf is fully cooked by inserting a knife into the centre – it should come out clean.

Remove from the oven, leave to cool and enjoy!

Tip
These also turn into tasty muffins if you divide the mixture among the 12 holes of a muffin tray lined with muffin cases (they'll take a little less time to cook). Don't forget to add chocolate chips for grown-ups and older children.

BREAKFAST

6+ MONTHS

Golden Porridge

Start the day right with this warming, spiced porridge that is as delicious as it is good for you. This vibrant twist combines the earthy warmth of turmeric with the sweet spice of cinnamon, offering a complex flavour profile for your baby. The addition of black pepper enhances the body's absorption of turmeric's active compound, curcumin, maximising its health benefits.

PREP: 5 minutes
COOK: 10 minutes

SERVES: 2 PEOPLE

- 300ml milk of choice
- ½ tsp turmeric
- ½ tsp ground cinnamon
- pinch of ground black pepper
- 30g rolled oats

Put the milk and spices in a saucepan and cook for about 5 minutes, allowing the milk to come to the boil.

Add the oats and cook for about 5 minutes over a medium heat, or until it reaches the desired consistency, stirring occasionally.

Tip
Add some grated courgette or carrot while cooking to sneak in some extra veggies.

9+ MONTHS

Blueberry Scones

A healthy bread that is crusty on the outside and fluffy on the inside which is sweetened with blueberries. You can use the crust as a resistive type of food for your baby to practise their oral-motor skills on. Offer the soft inside as your baby is getting to grips with finger foods.

PREP: 10 minutes
COOK: 25–30 minutes

MAKES: 7–8 SCONES

- 225g full-fat unsweetened Greek yoghurt
- 100g blueberries
- 200g plain flour
- 2 tsp baking powder
- 1 tsp ground cinnamon (optional)
- 1 egg, beaten, for egg wash (optional – can be substituted for milk wash)

Preheat the oven to 190°C and line a baking tray with baking parchment.

Mix the yoghurt and blueberries in a bowl and mix the flour, baking powder and cinnamon (if using) in a separate bowl, then add them to the yoghurt and blueberries. Knead with your fist briefly for 1–2 minutes to make a dough (add some extra flour if you feel it's too sticky, but be aware that too much kneading will make the scones tough and dense).

Divide the mixture with a spatula into 7 or 8 similar-sized pieces and roughly shape into circular scones before the mixture becomes too sticky.

Space out the scones on the lined baking tray, then brush them with the egg or some milk (this helps give them a golden colour).

Bake in the oven for 25–30 minutes, until golden brown, then remove and leave to cool on a wire rack. Enjoy with unsalted butter.

BREAKFAST

6+ MONTHS

Smoothie Bowl – Three Ways

Smoothie bowls are my immediate go-to on hot days, sick days and weekends, and I love how adaptable they are in terms of flavour and ingredients. Not to mention they are super quick to make, and most toddlers and babies love them, even through fussy phases.

If you have ever ordered a mango lassi at an Indian restaurant, you will know how divine they taste – a lassi never fails to quench my thirst, and neither does this sweet mango smoothie bowl. The peanut butter and banana is my absolute go-to if we are having some glorious sunshine, the children are poorly, or we just fancy a change at the weekend. Finally, if your little one loves Weetabix and you want to mix things up a little, try the iron rich, veggie-packed, 'Hulk' smoothie bowl to upgrade your average bowl of cereal.

If you forget to freeze a banana, you can use a room-temperature one and add some ice for a cooling effect. I always replace the frozen ripe banana in the freezer with a new one every time I use it, so I am prepared for the next time!

continued overleaf...

BREAKFAST

one

Super-green Weetabix Smoothie Bowl

PREP: 5 minutes

SERVES: 1 ADULT AND 1 BABY

- 2 Weetabix (or wheat biscuits)
- 1 banana, peeled, sliced and frozen
- small handful of spinach
- ½ ripe avocado, stoned and peeled
- splash of milk of choice
- desiccated coconut, to serve (optional)

Put all the ingredients in a blender and blend until smooth. Serve in bowls, sprinkled with some desiccated coconut for extra sweetness, if you like.

two

Mango Lassi

PREP: 5 minutes

SERVES: 1 ADULT AND 1 BABY

- 100g frozen or fresh mango
- 100g plain full-fat natural yoghurt
- 1 banana, peeled, sliced and frozen
- 2 tbsp rolled oats
- splash of milk of choice
- crushed pistachios, to serve (optional)

Put all the ingredients in a blender and blend until smooth. Serve in bowls with a sprinkle of crushed pistachios on top if you have them to hand.

Tip
For the best flavour, find your nearest Asian food shop that sells boxes of honey mangoes and you will not be disappointed!

BREAKFAST

three

Peanut Butter and Banana Smoothie Bowl

PREP: 5 minutes

SERVES: 1 ADULT AND 1 BABY

- 1 banana, peeled, sliced and frozen
- 2 tbsp rolled oats
- 2 tbsp full-fat unsweetened Greek yoghurt
- 1 tbsp chia seeds
- 1 tbsp smooth peanut butter
- splash of milk of choice

Put all the ingredients in a blender and blend until smooth. Serve in bowls.

Tip
A great way to allow your baby to practice self-feeding with a spoon.

Lunch

CHAPTER 5

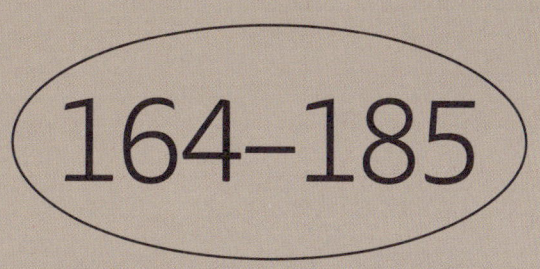

Lunch seems to be the meal that most parents struggle with as it often needs to be something quick and simple that can be eaten on the go. I know it can be hard to offer variety, as sandwiches and wraps tend to be a popular go-to, but I hope this section inspires you to add something different. The bonus is that most of the prep for some of the recipes can be done the night before to make it easier the next day.

Don't be hard on yourself if you are only managing to give your little one similar meals at lunchtime – just try to change up one thing a day, whether that's the bread, spread, veg or fruit. Also, there is no harm in putting 'picky' plates together with an array of leftover food from the fridge. It doesn't have to include ingredients you would traditionally serve together, so it might be hummus with broccoli and toast, for instance – it just makes life a little easier.

9+ MONTHS

Salmon Poke Bowl

I love a good poke bowl and find it so refreshing on those warmer sunnier days, so I created one we can eat as a family. It is super versatile, in that any of the fruit or veggies can be swapped for what you have in the fridge, so it's great for when you have leftover cooked fish or rice from the day before.

PREP: 5 minutes
COOK: 5 minutes

SERVES: 2 ADULTS AND 2 CHILDREN

- 250g packet microwave basmati rice
- 2 fillets of cooked salmon
- 1 mango, peeled, stoned and cubed
- 1 ripe avocado, stoned, peeled and diced or mashed
- ½ cucumber, diced
- 8–10 tomatoes, quartered (peeled if you like, for younger children)
- 1 carrot, peeled and grated

FOR THE PEANUT BUTTER YOGHURT SAUCE
- 2 tbsp plain full-fat natural yoghurt
- 1 tsp smooth peanut butter

Cook the rice according to the packet instructions.

Combine the yoghurt and peanut butter to make the sauce.

Assemble the poke bowl with all the components – you may want to serve the foods separately for baby to explore, or mash some of the salmon, rice and sauce together and offer it on a pre-loaded spoon, depending on your baby's preference (or do both!).

Serve with soy sauce and srirarcha for grown-ups.

Swap...
- salmon for any cooked fish (such as tuna) or chicken
- rice for any cooked grains
- mango for any citrus/juicy fruit
- veggies for what you have in the fridge

Tips
If you are serving to a younger baby, cut foods into narrow batons instead of dicing them, and remove skins.

6+ MONTHS

Tandoori-style Chicken Drumsticks

This 'prep and forget' recipe allows for the gently spiced marinade to come together in minutes either the night before or while your baby naps. The natural tanginess of the yoghurt tenderises the chicken and adds a gentle flavour on tiny tummies. Serving it on the bone is a fun way for baby to explore as they suck on the juicy chicken. This is ideal if baby does not have any teeth in the early days of weaning to avoid tearing off any chunks of meat. If you are worried about this, don't worry – finely shredding is a perfectly good option.

PREP: 10 minutes, plus marinating time
COOK: 40 minutes

SERVES: 2 ADULTS AND 2 CHILDREN

- 1kg chicken drumsticks
- 1 tbsp olive oil

FOR THE MARINADE
- ¼ tsp chilli powder
- 1½ tsp mild sweet paprika
- 1 tsp turmeric
- 1 tsp ground cumin
- 1 tsp garlic granules
- 2 tsp ground coriander
- 2 tsp garam masala
- ½ tsp ground black pepper
- 200g plain full-fat natural yoghurt

Mix all the marinade ingredients in a large bowl, add the chicken drumsticks, mix them around with a spoon to coat them, cover and transfer to the fridge for at least 30 minutes (ideally overnight for more flavour). Preheat the oven to 180°C.

Lay the marinated drumsticks on a baking tray and bake in the oven for 40 minutes, until the juices run clear when you pierce the thickest part of the drumsticks.

Serve the drumsticks whole to your baby, removing any skin and loose bits of cartilage. If your baby may be able to tear bits off with their teeth, finely shred the chicken and mix it with rice and yoghurt to eat off a spoon.

9+ MONTHS

Ultimate French Toast – Three Ways

If you ask my eldest what he wants for lunch on a Sunday, the request is likely to be 'French toast'. It's a winner, especially when hosting or at a friend's house and a fabulous way to add some iron-rich protein to your sandwich!

If your little one has gone off egg, then it can be a great way to keep it in the diet, however if you want to make them without egg, you can dip them in your milk of choice then fry in unsalted butter instead of olive oil.

I find this a great way to sneak in variety as you can opt for savoury options such as peanut butter as well as sweet options such as fruit. It can be a nutritious option for any meal of the day, especially a lazy weekend (most of ours!) or a weeknight dinner. As it is similar looking to toast, it tends to be well-accepted in our household. I have listed our top three favourite combinations but there are many more!

continued overleaf...

one

Pizza French Toast

PREP: 5–10 minutes
COOK: 5 minutes

EACH RECIPE MAKES FOUR FINGER SLICES.

- 2 tbsp pizza sauce (or 1 tbsp tomato purée diluted with 1 tbsp water)
- pinch of dried mixed herbs
- handful of grated cheddar cheese
- 2 or 3 large spinach leaves (or toppings of choice)
- 2 slices of bread from a white loaf with wholegrain (also known as 50/50 or 'best of both'), crusts removed
- 1 egg, beaten
- 30ml milk of choice
- olive oil, for drizzling

Put the pizza sauce, herbs, cheese and spinach on a slice of bread then place the other slice of bread on top like a sandwich. Roll the sandwich with a rolling pin to flatten it then slice it into 4 fingers.

Whisk the egg and milk together in a shallow bowl until smooth, then dip the sandwich fingers into the egg mixture until fully coated.

Heat a little olive oil in a frying pan over a medium heat, then fry each finger for a couple of minutes on each side until golden brown and fully cooked.

Tip
These are best eaten on the day they are made and are a good option for lunch on-the-go.

two

Strawberry and Cream Cheese French Toast

- 1½ tbsp cream cheese
- 3 strawberries, hulled and mashed
- 2 slices of bread from a white loaf with wholegrain (also known as 50/50 or 'best of both'), crusts removed
- 1 egg, beaten
- 30ml milk of choice
- olive oil, for drizzling

Combine the cream cheese and mashed strawberries in a bowl. Spread the mixture on one slice of bread then place the other slice of bread on top like a sandwich. Roll the sandwich with a rolling pin to flatten it then slice it into 4 fingers.

Whisk the egg and milk together in a shallow bowl until smooth, then dip the sandwich fingers into the egg mixture until fully coated.

Heat a little olive oil in a frying pan over a medium heat, then fry each finger for a couple of minutes on each side until golden brown and fully cooked.

three

Peanut Butter and Banana French Toast

- ½ ripe banana, peeled and mashed
- 1 tbsp smooth peanut butter
- 2 slices of bread from a white loaf with wholegrain (also known as 50/50 or 'best of both'), crusts removed
- 1 egg, beaten
- 30ml milk of choice
- olive oil, for drizzling

Mix the mashed banana and peanut butter in a bowl. Spread the mixture on one slice of bread then place the other slice of bread on top like a sandwich. Roll the sandwich with a rolling pin to flatten it then slice it into 4 fingers.

Whisk the egg and milk together in a shallow bowl until smooth, then dip the sandwich fingers into the egg mixture until fully coated.

Heat a little olive oil in a frying pan over a medium heat, then fry each finger for a couple of minutes on each side until golden brown and fully cooked.

7+ MONTHS

Sweetcorn Tagliatelle

It can be hard to pack sweetcorn into meals during weaning as the kernels tend to be a choking hazard. I have never found them particularly easy to squish when you are short on time. This recipe is a great way to incorporate sweetcorn into a creamy garlicky pasta sauce, for an easy lunch or weeknight dinner, and it adds a natural sweetness.

PREP: 5 minutes
COOK: 15 minutes

SERVES: 2 ADULTS AND 2 CHILDREN

- 200g tagliatelle
- 1 tbsp olive oil
- 2 garlic cloves, chopped
- 1 leek, trimmed and roughly chopped
- 200g tin sweetcorn (no salt), drained
- 150ml milk of choice
- 50g ricotta cheese

Cook the tagliatelle in a saucepan of boiling water.

Meanwhile, heat the olive oil in a frying pan over a medium heat. Add the garlic and chopped leek and cook for 4–5 minutes until soft. Add the sweetcorn and cook for further 3–4 minutes. Add the milk and ricotta cheese and stir until the all the cheese has melted into the milk.

Transfer the mixture from the pan to a blender with a splash of the pasta cooking water and blend until smooth (or blend with a stick blender in the pan).

Drain the pasta, return it to the saucepan, then pour in the sauce from the blender or frying pan and heat through to serve.

6+ MONTHS

Masala Beans

Who doesn't love baked beans? This is a great and quick way to introduce new flavours using a familiar and budget-friendly store-cupboard ingredient. These beans are best served with warm, buttered toast fingers. Feel free to add a bit more spice or chilli powder to your portion.

PREP: 5 minutes
COOK: 5 minutes

SERVES: 2 ADULTS AND 2 CHILDREN

- 1 garlic clove, roughly chopped
- 1 medium onion, peeled and roughly chopped
- 1 tbsp olive oil
- ½ tsp ground cumin
- 2 tsp garam masala
- ½ tsp freshly ground black pepper
- ¼ tsp mild chilli powder (optional)
- 2 x 400g tins baked beans (low salt and low sugar)
- handful of fresh coriander, finely chopped

Put the garlic and onion in a blender and blend to make a paste.

Heat the olive oil in a saucepan over a medium heat. Add the onion and garlic and cook, stirring, until it starts to brown, then add the cumin, garam masala, black pepper and chilli powder and fry for a couple of minutes until aromatic. Add the baked beans and coriander and cook for about 5 minutes until heated through.

Mash the beans with a fork before serving (<12 months), as they can be a choking hazard.

Tip
You can dip toast fingers in the sauce to soften them further and offer the mashed beans by pre-loading them on the spoon or squashing them onto the toast finger.

Lentil and Potato Flatbread

7+ MONTHS

ALOO PARATHA

If you are looking for a delicious lentil-based finger food that uses only a handful of ingredients and saves the mess of lentil curries, then this one is for you. The flatbreads are a fabulous way for vegetarian and vegan families to get some iron into their little ones.

PREP: 5 minutes
COOK: 35 minutes

MAKES: 6-8 PANCAKES

- 1 large floury potato (about 300g), peeled and cut into chunks
- 75g red lentils, rinsed (soak overnight if possible, to aid digestion)
- 3 tbsp plain flour or wholewheat flour
- 1 tsp mild sweet paprika
- 1 tsp freshly ground black pepper
- ½ tsp ground cumin
- knob of unsalted butter or 1-2 tbsp olive oil

Tips
If the mixture seems too wet or you accidentally add too much water, you can cover it and leave to stand for 15 minutes or add more flour.

Cook the potato and red lentils in a saucepan of boiling water for 20-25 minutes.

Once you can easily pierce the potato with a fork, drain thoroughly and transfer the cooked potato and lentils to a dish. Add the flour and spices while the potato and lentils are still warm, then mash until everything is fully combined and you have a smooth dough. Add a splash more water if the dough seems too dry – it will make it easier to handle and roll.

Divide the mixture evenly into 6-8 pieces and roll the pieces of dough into balls with your hands. Flatten them to a thickness of 3-5mm using a rolling pin or your hands (if rolling them with a rolling pin, you might need to dust the worktop with flour).

Heat the butter or oil in a frying pan over a high heat then cook the flatbreads for 2-3 minutes on each side, flipping them with a spatula.

Brush the cooked breads with extra melted unsalted butter for added moisture/healthy fats and enjoy them dipped in natural yoghurt.

7+ MONTHS

Veggie-loaded Muffins

Savoury muffins are a great option for on-the-go lunch or snacks when you are out and about and need something that's not too messy. These veg-packed muffins contain yoghurt to make them moist and quinoa for extra fibre and minerals such as magnesium, iron and zinc.

PREP: 15 minutes
COOK: 30 minutes

MAKES: 12 MUFFINS

- 50g quinoa
- 1 carrot
- 1 courgette
- 100g full-fat unsweetened Greek yoghurt
- 2 eggs
- 1 tsp dried oregano
- 100g self-raising flour
- 80g tinned, drained, unsalted sweetcorn, squished
- 15g cheddar cheese, grated (optional)

Preheat the oven to 190°C and grease a 12-hole muffin tin with butter or oil.

Cook the quinoa in a saucepan of 200ml boiling water for 15 minutes, or according to the packet instructions.

Meanwhile, grate the carrot and courgette and pat them dry with a tea towel or thick kitchen paper.

Mix the wet ingredients together (the yoghurt and eggs) in a bowl and whisk with a fork until well combined. Mix in the grated veggies, corn and oregano, then add the dry ingredients (the flour and cooked quinoa) and mix until combined.

Pour the mix into the greased muffin tin (about 2 heaped tablespoons per muffin) and sprinkle cheese on top of each muffin (if using). Bake for 25–30 minutes until well risen.

Remove from the oven and leave them in the tin to cool for at least 30 minutes before serving.

Tip
You can substitute the quinoa for plain flour if you have none in the cupboard.

LUNCH

7+ MONTHS

Sweet Potato and Black Bean Quesadillas

This is one of our family's favourite comforting lunches – it's like being in cheesy bean heaven! It comes together really quickly with leftover Sweet Potato and Black Bean Mash in the fridge (page 135). If you are starting from scratch, use the short version to save time for a speedy weeknight dinner.

PREP: 5 minutes
COOK: 10–15 minutes

SERVES: 2 ADULTS AND 2 CHILDREN

- olive oil, for drizzling
- 4 wholemeal wraps
- Approx. 150g Sweet Potato and Black Bean Mash (page 135)
- 60g cheddar cheese, grated (optional)

Heat a little olive oil in a large frying pan over a medium-high heat. Place a wrap flat in the pan, add sweet potato and black bean mash to one side of the wrap, sprinkle some of the cheese on top (if using) then fold over the wrap to enclose the filling. Flip the wrap after 1 or 2 minutes so the other side is cooked and the mash inside is warmed through.

Slice into fingers for baby and triangles for toddlers/grown-ups.

Tip
If your toddler or baby isn't keen on black beans, you can gradually introduce them by using a much higher potato-to-bean ratio to begin with then slowly, over time, increase the proportion of black beans.

6+ MONTHS

Pistachio Pesto Pasta

This is a weekly staple in our house, and it's a great way to introduce and maintain pistachio in the diet – they add a natural creamy sweetness to the pesto. If you like, you can alternate between using pistachio, pine nuts or pre-soaked cashew nuts.

PREP: 5 minutes
COOK: 10 minutes

SERVES: 2 ADULTS AND 1 BABY

- 200g rigatoni
- 50g fresh basil leaves
- 50g unsalted pistachio kernels
- 25g Parmesan cheese, grated
- 50ml olive oil

Cook your pasta according to the packet instructions.

While the pasta is cooking, put the basil, pistachios, Parmesan and olive oil in a blender and blend until smooth.

Drain the pasta, leaving a splash of pasta cooking water in the pan, and add the pesto to the pan with the pasta, stirring it over the heat for a couple of minutes.

Serve with veggies – yes, it really is as easy and as quick as that!

Tip
When making pesto (or any pasta sauce), batch cook it and freeze it in ice-cube trays so that when you cook pasta, you can defrost the cubes rather than having to make the sauce from scratch every time.

6+ MONTHS

Vegan Pancakes

This allergy-friendly recipe uses gluten-free chickpea flour to create an irresistible spiced savoury pancake without needing milk or eggs. It is packed with veggies and is super flexible – feel free to swap the veggies for whatever you have to hand. You can use plain wheat flour instead of chickpea flour if that's all you have to hand.

PREP: 5–10 minutes
COOK: 8 minutes

MAKES: 10–12 PANCAKES

- 200g gram flour (also known as chickpea flour or 'besan')
- 1 carrot, grated
- ½ courgette, grated
- 1 small onion, diced
- ½ tsp ground coriander
- ½ tsp ground cumin
- ½ tsp garam masala
- 300ml water
- olive oil, for drizzling

In a bowl, mix the flour, carrot, courgette, onion and spices. Add 250ml of the water and mix: the mixture should be runny, so add the remaining 50ml of water if needed. You don't want to add too much water as it will cause the pancakes to fall apart in the pan when you try to flip them.

Heat a drizzle of olive oil in a frying pan over a medium-low heat, add 2–3 tbsp of the mixture and spread it out thinly with the back of a large spoon. Cook for about 2 minutes, then flip the pancake and cook for a further 2 minutes until it is cooked through. Remove from the pan and continue cooking the rest of the mixture.

Serve warm, with a yoghurt dip (such as my Raita on page 237).

6+ MONTHS

Scrambled Cottage Cheese

This was inspired by one of my childhood favourite dishes, paneer bhurji, which is essentially Indian cottage cheese and veggies. It takes hours to make from scratch – I remember watching my mother boil milk to make the cheese and then strain it with a cheesecloth. I use shop-bought cottage cheese for a simpler version and it works as a quick breakfast or lunch.

PREP: 5 minutes
COOK: 10–15 minutes

SERVES: 2 ADULTS AND 2 CHILDREN

- 300g cottage cheese
- 1 tbsp olive oil
- 1 onion, chopped
- 1 plum tomato, skinned and finely chopped
- ¼ tsp turmeric
- ½ tsp garam masala
- 100g frozen peas
- handful of chopped fresh coriander (optional)

Rinse the cottage cheese with cold water if you want to reduce the salt content. Drain.

Heat the olive oil in a frying pan over a medium heat, add the onion, tomato, turmeric and garam masala and sauté for 5 minutes until soft. Add the cottage cheese and peas and cook for a further 5 minutes. Turn off the heat and stir in the chopped coriander (if using), then serve.

Tip
Crack in 1 egg when you add the cottage cheese, for extra nutrition. You can substitute the cottage cheese for crumbled paneer for a truly authentic taste!

6+ MONTHS

Immune-supporting Orange and Lentil Orzo Soup

This soupy vegan dish was created on cold winter's day when the cupboards were looking empty and I needed to whip up lunch. It is packed with carotenoids to support healthy vision and skin. The vitamin C packed veggies help to absorb iron from the lentils. It's a great pick-me-up during illness.

PREP: 5–10 minutes
COOK: 25 minutes

SERVES: 2 ADULTS AND 2 CHILDREN

- 100g red lentils, rinsed and drained
- 500ml vegetable stock (no-/low-salt vegetable stock cube dissolved in 500ml water)
- 1 carrot
- ½ red pepper, deseeded
- 85g orzo
- 200ml water
- 400g tin chopped tomatoes
- 1 tsp dried mixed herbs
- 1 tsp freshly ground black pepper
- 30g cheddar cheese, grated (optional – leave it out if keeping the dish vegan)
- handful of chopped coriander, to serve (optional)

Par-cook the lentils in the stock in a saucepan for 15 minutes (or according to the packet instructions).

Meanwhile, grate the carrot and finely dice the red pepper. Add these to the pan of par-cooked lentils and let them soften for a minute or so, then add the chopped tomatoes and simmer for 5 minutes until reduced. Add the orzo and 200ml water and stir to ensure the orzo doesn't clump at the bottom of the pan, then add the mixed herbs, black pepper and cheese for creaminess (if using).

Top with chopped coriander and serve with a further side of grated carrot and quartered cherry tomatoes for baby to explore.

Tip
Add an extra 30g of grated cheddar cheese, once you have taken baby's portion out, for extra creaminess for the whole family.

Dinner

CHAPTER 6

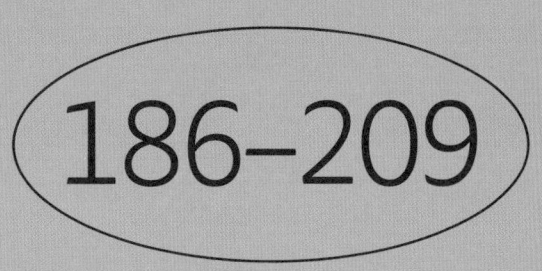

I know some people say that breakfast is the most important meal of the day, but for me it is definitely dinner! I look forward to something hearty, warm and wholesome at the end of a long day that can be eaten and enjoyed by the whole family. These are my favourite meals and, although a handful of them may take longer to prepare, this is my 'self-care' in terms of cooking something comforting and satisfying, not only for my family but for myself too. I have also created much quicker versions of authentic traditional recipes in line with modern-day living and you'll be surprised how some of them can come together in minutes and still taste like a gourmet dish. I hope you enjoy them as much as my family and I do.

7+ MONTHS

Baby Butter Chicken Curry

This is one of my original social media recipes and a firm favourite in many households. This recipe creates a creamy, indulgent, buttery chicken curry which is ideal if you want to offer your baby a higher-calorie meal. These gentle but delicious flavours will have grown-ups going back for more too – I love to make this if we have guests coming over.

PREP: 10 minutes
COOK: 20–25 minutes

SERVES: 2 ADULTS AND 2 CHILDREN

- 500g boneless, skinless chicken thighs

FOR THE MARINADE
- 3 tbsp full-fat unsweetened Greek yoghurt
- 1 tsp ground cumin
- 1 tsp garam masala
- 1 tsp turmeric
- 1 tsp mild sweet paprika
- 2 garlic cloves, crushed
- 2.5cm piece of ginger, grated

FOR THE SAUCE
- 1 tbsp olive oil
- 2 tbsp butter
- 1 medium onion, diced
- 1 tsp ground cumin
- 1 tsp ground coriander
- 1 tsp garam masala
- 2 garlic cloves, crushed
- 2 cm piece of ginger, grated
- 400g tomato passata
- 200ml double cream

Mix all the marinade ingredients in a bowl, add the chicken and leave to marinate for at least 15 minutes (or for a few hours/overnight in the fridge).

While chicken is marinating, heat the oil and butter in a large saucepan over a medium heat. Add the onion and cook for 5–10 minutes until softened and becoming translucent. Add the marinated chicken and cook until it starts to brown slightly, then add the spices and cook for a couple of minutes until aromatic. Add the garlic and ginger and cook for another minute or two until aromatic then add the tomato passata. If it looks dry, add 50mls of water. Mix and cook for about 5-10 minutes to allow it to reduce.

Add the double cream, mix and cook for 5–10 minutes until the sauce reaches the desired thickness, then remove from the heat and use two forks to finely shred the chicken.

Serve with rice, naan, yoghurt and vegetables. Blend baby's portion if you want a smooth consistency.

7+ MONTHS

Mini Sweet Potato Pizzas

If you find you are constantly relying on bread for lunch and want to make your own pizza base, try sweet potato as a nutritious alternative. It is a rich, natural source of vitamin C and fibre, and it helps the body to produce vitamin A. Add your favourite toppings – I love roasted veggies on mine.

PREP: 5–10 minutes
COOK: 25 minutes

MAKES: 2 MINI PIZZAS

- 1 large sweet potato
- olive oil, for drizzling
- 1 tsp dried oregano
- 4 tbsp low-salt pizza sauce
- 15g grated cheddar cheese or mozzarella
- ½ courgette, diced or grated
- 4–5 mushrooms, chopped

Tip
If you prefer to make your own sauce, use 1 tbsp tomato purée, 2 tbsp water and ¼ tsp oregano to spread on one pizza. The home-made sauce takes under 5 minutes to make and is delightful.

Preheat the oven to 220°C.

Wash the sweet potato and prick it with a fork. Wrap it in a sheet of kitchen paper and cook in the microwave on High for 3 minutes, then turn it over and cook for a further 2 minutes (or bake it in a hot oven until cooked through).

Unwrap the sweet potato, put it on a sheet of baking parchment and cut it in half (keeping the skin on). Put another sheet of parchment over the potato halves and squash each half using a frying pan to a thickness of roughly 2–3mm. Remove the top sheet of parchment and drizzle each squashed half with olive oil and sprinkle with oregano.

Transfer the sweet potato pizza bases (on the baking parchment) to the oven and bake for 10 minutes.

Remove from the oven and spread the pizza sauce over the bases. Add the cheese and vegetables and return to the oven for a further 10 minutes.

Remove from the oven, slice into pizza fingers and serve.

7+ MONTHS

One-pot Veggie Orzo

A hands-off weeknight, one-pot dinner because who doesn't love to save on the washing up? It resembles a cheat's risotto as I rarely have time to cook proper risotto since having children. The texture is soft for early weaners and the comforting cheesy flavour tends to go down well with toddlers too.

PREP: 10 minutes
COOK: 30–35 minutes

SERVES: 2 ADULTS AND 2 CHILDREN

- ½ head broccoli florets, finely chopped
- ½ onion, finely chopped
- 80g mushrooms, finely chopped
- 250g cherry tomatoes
- olive oil, for drizzling
- dried mixed herbs, to taste
- 250g orzo
- 500ml chicken stock (1 no-/low-salt chicken stock cube dissolved in 500ml water)
- 60g cheddar cheese, grated

Preheat the oven to 190°C.

Put the broccoli, onion, mushrooms and cherry tomatoes in a large baking dish with plenty of olive oil and some mixed herbs then combine. Roast in the oven for 10–12 minutes.

Remove the dish from the oven and add the orzo and stock. Sprinkle more dried herbs on top and mix the contents of the dish together. Cover the dish with foil and place back in the oven for 20–30 minutes, stirring once or twice to ensure the orzo doesn't stick to the bottom of the dish and adding 100ml water if it starts to look dry or clumpy.

Remove the dish from the oven, uncover, stir, and add splash of water to loosen if needed. Squish all the cherry tomatoes for extra juice and to avoid them becoming a choking hazard, and stir in the grated cheese for ultra-creaminess – it will melt into the sauce.

Ensure all tomato skin is removed from your baby's portion for serving. Any larger pieces of vegetables such as broccoli can be placed on the side as finger food to make it easier for baby to handle.

Tip
Add some cooked boneless fish if you want to increase the protein content of this dish.

7+ MONTHS

Quick Kidney Bean Curry

RAJMA

This heart-warming vegan Indian dish is a great source of protein as well as two other essential nutrients: iron and zinc. It was one of my favourite childhood meals, but traditionally it takes hours to cook. I have adapted it to create a speedy version for busy families that takes less than 30 minutes from start to finish. Serve this soupy recipe with rice and yoghurt.

PREP: 5 minutes
COOK: 22 minutes

SERVES: 4 PEOPLE

- 2 tbsp olive oil
- 2 garlic cloves, crushed
- 2.5cm piece of ginger, grated
- 400g tin finely chopped tomatoes
- 400ml tin coconut milk
- 400g tin red kidney beans, drained and rinsed
- large handful of chopped coriander

In a large pan, heat the oil over a medium heat. Add the garlic and ginger and cook for 1–2 minutes until aromatic.

Add the tomatoes, coconut milk, kidney beans and garam masala. Cook for 20 minutes, stirring regularly.

Remove from the heat and stir in the chopped coriander. Serve with rice and yoghurt.

Tip
Mash the beans before serving until around 12 months of age or whenever you are happy your little one can handle them.

7+ MONTHS

Salmon Fishcakes

If you want to mix up the classic Simple Salmon, Broccoli and Potato dish (page 128) then this is a great finger food option once your little one has got into the swing of of self-feeding. It also doubles up as a mess-free lunch or snack on the go. Salmon is rich in omega-3 fatty acids, so I love taking the leftovers to work as 'brain' food!

PREP: 10 minutes (while salmon cooking)
COOK: 30 minutes

MAKES: APPROXIMATELY 14–16 FISHCAKES

- 250g skinless salmon fillets (about 2 fillets)
- 500g sweet potato (about 2 potatoes)
- 75g bread (I use a white loaf with wholegrain, also known as 50/50 or 'best of both') or breadcrumbs
- 1 egg, beaten
- handful of finely chopped parsley
- juice of ½ lemon
- olive oil, for drizzling
- Smashed Peas (page 243), to serve

Tip
Always check the salmon for bones before mashing into the recipe as they can be a choking hazard.

Preheat the oven to 200°C.

Bake the salmon fillets on a baking tray in the oven for 18–20 minutes until cooked through but still tender.

While the salmon is cooking, pierce the sweet potatoes all over, place in a microwavable bowl then put in the microwave and cook for 5 minutes then turn them over and microwave for another 5 minutes (or cook them in a hot oven until cooked through). Cut them in half and scoop out the cooked sweet potato from the skin.

Blitz the bread in a blender to make breadcrumbs (if not using ready-made breadcrumbs).

In a mixing bowl, combine the sweet potato flesh, breadcrumbs, egg, parsley and lemon juice. Mash in the cooked salmon, then roll the mixture into about 16 balls and flatten them into circular patties.

Heat a drizzle of olive oil in a frying pan over a medium heat, then fry the fishcakes for 2–3 minutes on each side, and serve with the smashed peas.

Tray-bake Chicken Fajita

I love a Mexican-style fajita feast but once I discovered I could make them in the oven and leave them to do their thing rather than standing over the cooker, it got even better! Have fun with the sides and offer them in a buffet style to your family so everyone can put their own stamp on it – your baby will need a little help though.

PREP: 5 minutes
COOK: 30–35 minutes

SERVES: 4–5 PEOPLE

- 1 onion, cut into wedges
- 2 red peppers, deseeded and cut into batons
- olive oil, for drizzling
- 500g boneless, skinless chicken thighs

FOR THE SPICE MIX
- 2 tsp ground cumin
- 1 tsp mild sweet paprika
- 1 tsp dried oregano
- 1 tsp garlic granules
- ½ tsp freshly ground black pepper

TO SERVE
- 4 or 5 buttered wholewheat tortilla wraps, warmed through
- home-made Cuca-mole (page 241)
- 60g cheddar cheese, grated
- sour cream, to taste

Preheat the oven to 200°C and combine the spices for the spice mix.

Put the onion and peppers in a baking tray, drizzle generously with olive oil, add the chicken thighs and season with the spice mix. Bake in the oven for 30 minutes, or until the chicken is fully cooked and the juices run clear when you pierce the thickest part of the thighs with a knife.

Serve each element of the dish separately (deconstructed) to your baby, with buttered wholewheat tortilla wraps, shredded chicken, cuca-mole, cheese and sour cream.

Tips
Cut up large pieces of chicken to help it cook quicker on the heat and finely shred it when serving to your baby. You can use chicken breast but we prefer thigh as it is much more tender and flavoursome.

7+ MONTHS

One-pot Lasagne

Lasagne is a firm favourite in our household, but we rarely have time to make it the traditional way. This is how my one-pot lasagne was born, a lamb-mince version of the dish which can easily be made in a little over 30 minutes. It is full of iron and protein and still has all the comforting flavours of an authentic lasagne using ingredients that are baby-friendly.

PREP: 5 minutes
COOK: 25–30 minutes

SERVES: A FAMILY OF 4, WITH LEFTOVERS

- 2tbsp olive oil
- 400g minced lamb
- 5 tsp dried oregano
- 2 garlic cloves, crushed
- 700g tomato passata
- 1 no-/low-salt vegetable stock cube
- 100mls water
- 4 dried lasagne sheets
- 60g fresh mozzarella, chopped
- Handful of chopped parsley

Heat the olive oil in a frying pan over a medium heat, add the lamb mince and cook while breaking it up with a wooden spoon. After 3–4 minutes, add 3 tsp dried mixed oregano and the crushed garlic then stir. Once the lamb mince has fully browned after 8–9 minutes, add the tomato passata and crumble in the veggie stock cube. Mix thoroughly then break up the lasagne sheets into small pieces and add to the pan with 100mls water, 3 tsp oregano and the mozzarella. Turn down the heat and bring to a simmer, then cover and cook for about 20 minutes until the sauce has reduced and you have reached the desired consistency. Serve with chopped parsley on top.

Tips
This is perfect for batch cooking. I often store it in little pots and defrost it for a quick lunch. You can add tinned lentils and less meat if you are on a budget or prefer a vegetarian option.

6+ MONTHS

Saag Tofu Vegan Curry

My twist on this classic Indian favourite makes it suitable for those with dairy allergies and provides an extra boost of iron from tofu. Tofu can be hard to flavour at times, so I much prefer to serve it in a curry sauce to create a rich taste. The curry is great with steamed rice and cucumber raita (see page 237).

PREP: 5 minutes
COOK: 25 minutes

SERVES: 2 ADULTS AND 2 CHILDREN

- 1 bag of fresh spinach (about 400g) or 150g frozen spinach
- olive oil, for drizzling
- 1 onion, roughly chopped
- 2 garlic cloves, roughly chopped
- 1cm piece of ginger, peeled and grated (optional)
- 200g tinned chopped tomatoes
- ½ tsp ground cumin
- ½ tsp turmeric
- ½ tsp freshly ground black pepper
- 1 x 400g packet of organic firm tofu
- knob of butter
- 2 tbsp plain natural yoghurt
- juice of ½ lemon
- 20g unsalted butter

Blanch the spinach (if using fresh) briefly in a pan of boiling water to wilt it, then drain and place it in a bowl of ice-cold water to halt the cooking process (and reduce any bitterness).

Heat a little olive oil in a large frying pan over a medium heat, add the onion, garlic and ginger and sauté for a few minutes until softened. Stir in the wilted spinach (or frozen spinach if using until warmed through), then transfer the mixture to a blender and blend until smooth. Put the mixture back in the pan, add the chopped tomatoes and simmer for 5–10 minutes until reduced. Add a little water if you like, to loosen the sauce.

Meanwhile, fry the spices in a generous drizzle of olive oil in a separate pan over a high heat. Add the chopped tofu and cook for a couple of minutes (or according to the packet instructions) until heated through, then add it to the curry mix and stir. Remove from the heat, add the butter, yoghurt and balance out the flavours with a gentle squeeze of lemon.

Serve the curry with the tofu crumbled, mashed or in narrow batons as finger food.

DINNER

Tip
Swap the tofu for paneer cheese for the indulgent traditional version if you prefer a dairy option or have a soy allergy.

7+ MONTHS

Hearty Mac 'n' Cheese

If you are looking for a comforting meal, this calcium-packed dish will be a sure-fire favourite with your little ones. My secret ingredients are butternut squash to add extra beta-carotene and cauliflower for a hidden veggie which adds a lovely creamy texture to the sauce. This means it can be made without the cheese and still taste delicious.

PREP: 5 minutes
COOK: 25 minutes

SERVES: 2 ADULTS AND 2 CHILDREN

- ½ small butternut squash, peeled, deseeded and cut into chunks
- ¼ large cauliflower, broken into florets
- 350g macaroni, or pasta of choice
- 50g unsalted butter
- 2 tbsp plain flour
- 300ml milk of choice
- 40g cheddar cheese, grated (optional)
- ½ tsp mild sweet paprika
- ½ tsp freshly ground black pepper
- 1 tbsp Dijon mustard (optional)

Cook the butternut squash and cauliflower in boiling water until soft then blend to a purée in a blender.

Cook your pasta of choice according to the packet instructions.

Meanwhile, melt the butter in a saucepan over a medium heat, add the flour and whisk to form a paste for a minute or so, to cook out the flour. Add the squash purée, spices and Dijon mustard (if using). Gradually pour in the milk, whisking continuously to keep the sauce smooth. Mix in the cheese if using it until melted. Add the macaroni to the pan with a splash of pasta sauce and stir. Serve with a side of veggies.

Swap

- For a dairy-free option, use olive oil instead of butter and a plant-based milk. Due to the creaminess of the cauliflower, cheese is not essential.

Tip
Set aside a cauliflower floret and butternut squash baton (before blending) to serve as a finger food for your baby. Make extra sauce to freeze for a busy day!

8+ MONTHS

Satay Noodles

It took us a long time to create a stir-fry sauce we could eat as a family, as our go-to usually involved soy sauce, honey and sriracha – all of which are not baby-friendly. After a bit of experimentation, we came up with this rich, creamy satay sauce that still has a bit of 'zing' and makes a super-speedy weeknight dinner. We tend to add prawns for extra protein.

PREP: 5 minutes
COOK: 10 minutes

SERVES: 3–4 PEOPLE

- olive oil, for drizzling
- 220g ready-prepared stir-fry vegetable mix (or whatever veggies you have in the fridge, cut into long batons)
- 150g raw peeled king prawns (optional)
- 275g packet stir-fry egg noodles

FOR THE SATAY SAUCE
- 2 tsp olive oil
- 2 tbsp smooth peanut butter
- 400g tin full-fat coconut milk
- 1 tsp mild curry powder
- juice of ½ lime

Heat a drizzle of olive oil in a frying pan over a high heat, add the vegetables sauté for 5–6 minutes.

While the vegetables are cooking, start to make the sauce: heat the olive oil in a saucepan over a medium heat and add the peanut butter. Mix to make a runny paste, then gradually stir in the coconut milk, about 100ml at a time, over a couple of minutes. Stir in the curry powder and lime juice.

Add the prawns (if using) to the sautéed vegetables and cook for a couple of minutes before adding the noodles.

Once the sauce is simmering, add it to the pan of noodles and vegetables.

Serve to your baby as is or chop the noodles to pre-load onto a spoon and serve the veggies (and prawns) as finger food, slicing the prawns lengthways for baby to reduce the risk of choking.

7+ MONTHS

Speedy Curried Cod Rice

You will be amazed by how quickly you can make this gently spiced, perfectly tender curried cod rice with only four main ingredients. It all comes together in under 20 minutes with the bonus of being a one-pot dish – minimal washing up!

PREP: 5 minutes
COOK: 20 minutes

SERVES: 2-3 ADULTS AND 2 CHILDREN

- 4 tbsp olive oil
- 2 cod fillets, boneless and deskinned (about 250g in total)
- 250g basmati rice, rinsed
- 80g frozen peas
- 500ml chicken stock (no-/low-salt chicken stock cube dissolved in 500ml water)
- 2 tsp curry powder
- 200ml water
- handful of chopped coriander (optional)

Heat the oil in a pan over a medium heat. Add the rice, chicken stock and curry powder and cook for 7–8 minutes.

Add the frozen peas, cod fillets and 200ml of water then cover and cook for a further 12 minutes on medium-low heat until the water has evaporated and the cod is cooked through.

Remove from the heat, flake the cooked fish, stir in the chopped coriander and leave to stand for 5–10 minutes for best results. Serve with plain natural yoghurt.

Tip
You can easily substitute the cod for salmon fillets if you prefer or use alternative veggies.

6+ MONTHS

Hidden Veg, Tofu and Chicken Curry

If you and your family are new to curries, this mild and flavoursome chicken is a good one to start with and has the consistency of a korma. It is also ideal for batch cooking and freezing. While it's important to expose your little one to lots of different vegetable finger foods, it can be helpful to pack extra veg into sauces too, to boost nutrient intake.

PREP: 5–10 minutes
COOK: 50 minutes

SERVES: 3–4 PEOPLE

- 3 carrots, chopped into 2–3cm chunks
- 3 beef or plum tomatoes, quartered
- 3 red peppers, deseeded and quartered
- olive oil, for drizzling
- ½ tsp ground cumin
- ½ tsp ground coriander
- 1 tsp garam masala
- ½ tsp mild chilli powder (optional)
- 2 garlic cloves, peeled
- 280g block firm tofu
- handful of coriander
- 1 medium onion, diced
- 500g boneless, skinless chicken thighs, diced

Preheat the oven to 180°C.

Put the carrots, tomatoes and red peppers in an ovenproof dish, drizzle with a generous amount of oil and toss with the cumin, coriander and half the garam masala (and the chilli powder, if using). Roast for 30 minutes until softened.

Remove from the oven, allow to cool, then transfer to a blender with the garlic, tofu and coriander and blend to a smooth sauce.

Heat a drizzle of olive oil in a frying pan over a medium heat, add the onion and fry for a few minutes until translucent. Add the chicken with the remaining garam masala and, once it starts to brown, stir in the blended vegetable sauce. Add a splash of water if desired to thin the sauce. Cook for 10–15 minutes until chicken is cooked through. Shred the chicken with two forks and serve with your cooked grain of choice or flatbread.

Tip
You can roast the vegetables early to save time – this will reduce the cooking time to 15–20 minutes.

9+ MONTHS

Prawn Linguine

Linguine has to be my favourite pasta dish. What I love most about this recipe is how simple yet flavoursome it is. It makes a perfect midweek dinner accompanied by a fresh summer salad. Prawns have always been my favourite type of shellfish so it is the one I have consciously exposed my children to on a regular basis.

PREP: 5 minutes
COOK: 15 minutes

SERVES: 4 PEOPLE

- 160g of linguine
- 165g raw large/king prawns
- 2 spring onions, soft bits roughly chopped
- 2 crushed garlic cloves
- juice of ½ lemon
- handful of fresh parsley, chopped

Cook the pasta in boiling water according to the packet instructions.

While the pasta is cooking, cook the spring onions for about 1 minute in 2 tablespoons of olive oil in a separate pan.

Add the prawns and garlic and cook for about 5 minutes until the prawns are cooked.

Add in the pasta with a splash of pasta water and the lemon juice. Cook gently until it forms a sticky sauce.

Take off the heat and stir in the parsley.

Tip
The best way to serve prawn to young babies is to slice in half lengthways to make them long and narrow to avoid choking.

Puddings

CHAPTER >

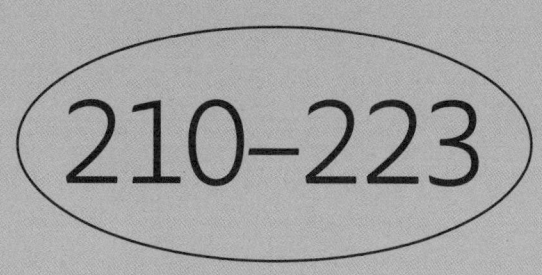

Puddings are something you may want to introduce to your baby a little later down the line when they are established on three meals a day and you start to notice their appetite for solids increasing. By no means do you need to serve puddings after every meal; however, if you find that you and your little one are getting tired of fruit and yoghurt, here are some ideas of delicious sugar-free puddings which can be enjoyed by the whole family.

Most of the prep for these recipes has been designed to take under 10 minutes using household staple ingredients, so they don't need to be planned ahead, but you may surprise yourself and find a little pocket of time during your baby's nap. They can also mostly be left to cook in the oven with a hands-off approach. Puddings can be a great way of getting in extra nutrients, and you can always add a sprinkle of sugar for older children or grown-ups.

Rice Pudding (KHEER)

You won't believe this rice pudding has no refined sugar in once you taste it, and it will leave you wanting more of the creamy comforting flavours. The fragrant but delicate cardamom combined with the natural sweetness from the blueberry compote just works and feels very light on the digestive system after a meal.

PREP: 5 minutes
COOK: 30 minutes

SERVES: 4 PEOPLE

- 100g basmati rice
- 400g tin full-fat coconut milk
- 500ml milk of choice
- ½ tsp ground cardamom
- handful of blueberries

Soak the rice in a bowl of cold water for about 10 minutes while you heat the milk.

Meanwhile, pour the coconut milk and milk into a saucepan and bring to the boil.

Rinse and drain the soaked rice and add it to the saucepan, reduce the heat to a simmer, stir and cook for 15–20 minutes, keeping an eye on it to make sure it doesn't boil over and stirring it occasionally. Add the ground cardamom (if using) and cook for a further 10 minutes, stirring if needed, until the rice is soft and creamy.

Put the blueberries in a microwaveable dish, cover and microwave on High for 30–60 seconds until they start to break down. Pour the blueberries over individual bowls of rice pudding.

Tip
Traditionally, kheer is served with nuts and raisins. Feel free to add this your dish and sprinkle ground nuts onto your baby's pudding.

PUDDINGS

12+ MONTHS

No-bake Mini Oat Cheesecakes

I will never forget the smile on the face of my eldest when I first made this for him as a toddler – he must have eaten three in a row. Another sugar-free, naturally sweet dessert which makes mini cheesecakes that are just the right size for little hands to hold.

PREP: 10–15 minutes, plus freezing time

MAKES: 6 MINI CHEESECAKES

- 80g rolled oats
- 25g unsalted butter
- 1 ripe banana, peeled
- 6 tbsp full-fat unsweetened Greek yoghurt
- 150g cream cheese

OPTIONAL TOPPINGS
- blueberries, strawberries, mango (cut the toppings appropriately for baby's age)

Put the oats and butter in a blender and blend until well combined. You may need to scrape down the sides of the bowl a couple of times to make sure everything's blended.

Divide the mixture among 6 muffin cases or 6 holes in a silicone muffin tray and flatten it with the back of a spoon. Place in the fridge.

Mash the banana in a mixing bowl until smooth, then add the yoghurt and stir until combined. Add the cream cheese and stir again to combine.

Remove the chilled bases from the fridge and spoon the cheesecake mixture on top of each base. Smooth the top and add your or your baby's preferred toppings. Freeze for 1 hour, then remove and enjoy!

Tip
You can make these for smaller babies without the oat base if it's too crunchy.

9+ MONTHS

Baby Cake Slice

These cake slices have a lovely soft texture and are a fabulous home-made baby pudding or snack which can even triple up as an on-the-go breakfast. I always end up eating half of these as snacks too, as they are so addictive and great for a slow release of energy, to help curb hunger.

PREP: 5 minutes
COOK: 20 minutes

SERVES: 1 ADULT AND 1 BABY

- 120g rolled oats (or instant oats)
- 2 ripe bananas, peeled
- 80g smooth peanut butter
- ½ tsp baking powder
- 120ml milk of choice, plus extra if needed

Preheat the oven to 180°C and grease or line a 21cm baking dish with baking parchment.

Put all the ingredients in a blender and blend until smooth, adding up to 80–100ml more milk to soften the mixture after blending.

Transfer to the lined dish and bake for 20 minutes until golden brown.

Remove from the oven, lift the cake out of the dish using the parchment paper and allow to cool for 5–10 minutes then slice and enjoy!

Tip
Try not to over-blend the mixture or it will become very dense. Add chocolate chips for older children – these are divine.

Crumble – Three Ways

Your little one is going to love these sugar-free crumbles, with their warming spices, and so will you! Serve them with natural yoghurt for baby. You won't even need to sweeten them for older children, especially if you use ripe fruit.

No-sugar Pear and Ginger Crumble

PREP: 10 minutes
COOK: 40 minutes

SERVES: 4–5 PEOPLE

- 4 ripe pears
- 1 tbsp olive oil or a knob of unsalted butter
- 1 tsp ground ginger
- 1 tsp ground nutmeg (optional)

FOR THE CRUMBLE MIX
- 240g oat flour
- 60g unsalted butter, melted
- 100ml milk of choice

Preheat the oven to 180°C and grease a round baking dish (about 23cm in diameter) with olive oil or butter.

First, make the crumble mix. Combine the oat flour, melted butter and milk in a bowl and stir or rub between your fingertips until well combined.

Peel and core the pears, then cut them into 1cm cubes.

Scatter the pear into the greased dish, spreading it out evenly. Sprinkle the pear with the spices, evenly scatter the crumble mix on top and bake for 40 minutes, until the pear is cooked and the crumble mix is golden.

Remove from the oven and leave to cool for at least 5–10 minutes to allow the oat topping to set before serving.

two

No-sugar Apple and Cinnamon Crumble

PREP: 10 minutes
COOK: 40 minutes

SERVES: 4–5 PEOPLE

- 4 dessert apples
- ½ teaspoon ground cinnamon

FOR THE CRUMBLE MIX

- 240g oat flour
- 60g unsalted butter, melted
- 100ml milk of choice

Preheat the oven to 180°C and grease a round baking dish (about 23cm in diameter) with olive oil or butter.

First, make the crumble mixture. Combine the oat flour, melted butter and milk in a bowl and stir or rub between your fingertips until well combined.

Peel and core the apples, then cut them into 1cm cubes.

Scatter the apple into the greased dish, spreading it out evenly. Sprinkle it with the cinnamon, evenly scatter the crumble mix on top and bake for 40 minutes, until the apple is cooked and the crumble mix is golden.

Remove from the oven and leave to cool for at least 5–10 minutes to allow the oat topping to set before serving.

three

No-sugar Berry Crumble

PREP: 10 minutes
COOK: 40 minutes

SERVES: 4–5 PEOPLE

- Crumble mix, as above
- 100g raspberries, squished
- 100g blueberries, squished
- juice of ½ lemon

Tip
Blend rolled oats to make oat flour or use Ready Brek as a great fortified option.

Preheat the oven to 180°C and grease a round baking dish (about 23cm in diameter) with olive oil or butter.

First, make the crumble mix as above.

Scatter the fruit into the greased dish, squeeze over the lemon juice and spread the fruit out out evenly. Scatter the crumble mix on top and bake for 40 minutes, until the crumble mix is golden.

Remove from the oven and leave to cool for at least 5–10 minutes to allow the oat topping to set before serving.

PUDDINGS

Jammie Chickpea Blondies

For years I have been adding hidden chickpeas to snacks such as pancakes, cookies and now these blondies. They are protein-packed, high in fibre and a great source of B vitamins amongst other minerals such as magnesium, iron and zinc.

PREP: 5 minutes
COOK: 30 minutes

MAKES: 12 BLONDIES

- 120g peanut butter
- 400g tin of chickpeas (rinsed and drained)
- 2 bananas
- 80g raspberries

Preheat oven to 180°C. Line a square oven-dish with parchment paper or grease with butter or oil.

Add all ingredients to a high-speed blender except the raspberries and blend until smooth.

Meanwhile, use a fork to mash the raspberries in a bowl and microwave for 60 seconds to make a quick jam (or use the raspberry chia jam recipe on page 245).

Spread half the blended mixture evenly in the oven-dish with a spatula and top with a layer of raspberry jam. Then spread the other half of the blended mixture on top.

Bake at 180°C for 30 minutes or until golden brown.

Leave to cool and slice into squares.

Tip
Add 2-3 tbsp of maple syrup to sweeten for older children or grown-ups. White chocolate chunks also work nicely.

6+ MONTHS

No-added-sugar Banana Bread

An improved version of one of my most viral recipes on social media. This is a bake that I would often make for playdates so grown-ups and babies can enjoy 'cake time' together without having to hide or restrict food. The natural sweetness from the ripe bananas means you don't even notice this recipe contains no added sugar.

PREP: 10 minutes
COOK: 25–30 minutes

**SERVES: 4–6 PEOPLE
(MAKES ABOUT 10 SLICES)**

- 110g rolled oats (or instant oats or oat flour)
- 3 large, ripe bananas, plus an extra banana peeled and halved lengthways to decorate (optional)
- 3 eggs, beaten
- ¾ tsp ground cinnamon
- 1 tsp baking powder
- 3 tbsp olive oil

Preheat the oven to 180°C and line the base and sides of a loaf tin with baking paper.

Put the oats in a blender and blend to make oat flour.

Mash the 3 bananas in a bowl until smooth, then add all the remaining ingredients – including the oat flour – and mix until well combined.

Transfer the mixture to the prepared loaf tin and place the banana slices on top (if using). Bake in the oven for 25–30 minutes, until a knife inserted into the centre of the bread comes out clean.

Remove from the oven, turn out of the tin and leave to cool for at least 15 minutes.

Tips
Add 1–2 handfuls of blueberries or raspberries to the mixture for extra sweetness. I find this one usually tastes better when cooled due to the oat flour in the recipe. If you want a 'cakier' texture then use plain flour instead of oat flour or 50:50.

Carrot Pudding

7+ MONTHS

HALWA

This iconic dish dates back to medieval times in India. Using only two household staple ingredients – carrots and milk – this recipe harnesses the natural sweetness of carrot and is packed with vitamins, minerals and fibre. You will be amazed at how, over time, the heat creates a sticky dessert without the need for any sugar or syrup.

PREP: 5 minutes
COOK: 20 minutes

SERVES: 4–6 PEOPLE

- olive oil, for drizzling
- 4 carrots, peeled and grated
- 500ml milk of choice
- 2 tbsp unsalted butter

Heat the olive oil in a large saucepan over a medium-high heat, add the grated carrots and cook for 10 minutes until soft.

Reduce the heat to medium, add the milk and cook for 10 minutes until the milk evaporates and the mixture is sticky. Stir in the butter just before all the milk has disappeared.

Remove from the heat and leave to cool a little before serving. Serve with banana nice cream (blend frozen banana) for a cooling effect.

Tip
You can add raisins, ground cardamom and ground almonds to serve, for an authentic flavour.

CHAPTER 8

Snacks and Dips

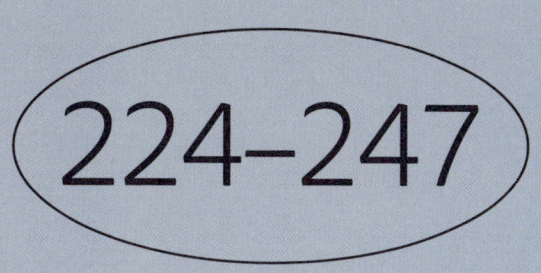

I have created this fun little section mostly for when your baby is approaching 12 months old and you may be thinking about adding in a mid-morning or mid-afternoon snack to their schedule. By no means are you expected to home-cook all snacks as well as three meals a day, but again I have focused on using household staple ingredients to create simple and enjoyable snacks without much faff.

Don't forget that snacks can be viewed as 'mini meals' and provide a great opportunity to add in extra nutrients, particularly if the meal before may not have gone as well as planned. I've also included a variety of dips that can be served alongside recipes such as fritters or crackers – these not only add variety, but are a great opportunity for your little one to develop their fine motor skills.

The recipes are designed to be batch cooked to last you a few days and they can be stored in the freezer for a busy day – your future self will be very thankful! They are also much cheaper than buying some of the marketed baby-/toddler-specific snacks which, of course, might be needed from time to time, but don't always offer much in the way of nutrition. These recipes can also be enjoyed by older children and are by no means 'baby' specific.

SNACKS AND DIPS

6+ MONTHS

ALOO GOBI

Spiced Cauliflower Potato Tots

These potato tots are inspired by the very simple Indian dish called aloo gobi (it literally means 'potato cauliflower'), a classic combination of ingredients that's simple but satisfies the palate. Rather than frying the tots, you just mash the ingredients together and bake them instead, with egg and cheese to bind them, making them easy for little hands to grab.

PREP: 10 minutes
COOK: 20 minutes

SERVES: 4 PEOPLE

- 300g floury potatoes (Maris Piper work well), peeled and cut into chunks
- 200g cauliflower (about ½ head of cauliflower), broken into florets
- 1 tbsp olive oil
- 1 tsp mild sweet paprika
- ½ tsp ground cumin
- 1cm piece of ginger, peeled and grated
- 1 egg, beaten
- 30g cheddar cheese, grated

Cook the potatoes and cauliflower in a saucepan of boiling water over a medium heat, covered with a lid, for 20 minutes until softened.

Remove the cauliflower 5 minutes before, cut off the stems and finely chop. Place into a microwavable dish and cook for 2 minutes.

Preheat the oven to 190°C and line a baking tray with baking parchment.

Take the pan off the heat and drain.

Mash the potato with olive oil until smooth then add the cooked cauliflower florets, spices, ginger, egg and cheese and mix together. Roll the mixture with your hands into little squares and place them on the lined baking tray, then bake in oven for 18–20 minutes, until golden.

Remove from the oven and leave to cool for at least 15 minutes, then serve to your baby.

Tip
If you have time, chill the mashed mixture before rolling it into squares – this will make it easier to handle and shape.

SNACKS AND DIPS

7+ MONTHS

Apple Oat Bars

Whenever I was out with other mums, I always saw how popular this store-bought snack was with tiny toddlers. While of course it is convenient, I wanted to make a home-made version that tasted just as delicious and was made with good-quality ingredients – now here it is! It doubles up perfectly as breakfast or a snack.

PREP: 5 minutes
COOK: 25 minutes

MAKES: 8-10 OAT BARS

- 1 large, ripe banana, peeled
- 2 large apples, peeled, cored and finely grated
- 120g rolled oats
- ½ tsp baking powder
- ½ tsp ground cinnamon
- 50ml milk of choice

Preheat the oven to 180°C and line a 21cm baking dish or lightly grease with butter or oil.

Mash the banana in a mixing bowl until smooth (or straight in the baking dish if you want to save on washing up). Add the grated apple, oats, baking powder and cinnamon and milk and mix until well combined. If mixture seems a little dry, add a splash more milk.

Transfer the mix to the baking dish, smooth out and bake in the oven for 25 minutes or until golden brown. Remove and leave to cool for at least 10 minutes before cutting into bars.

Tip
You could serve this with some thin, long slices of fresh apple for babies over 12 months or you can finely grate, steam or purée it for younger ones.

SNACKS AND DIPS

Fritters – Three Ways

Fritters remind me of the pakoras that my grandparents would usually serve with a cup of tea as a mid-afternoon snack. I tend to use chickpea flour, just as they did, as this flour has the added benefit of fibre and iron. They make the ideal finger food for your little ones and simply involve throwing everything into one bowl and frying until lovely and crispy. They are delicious plain but there are optional spices if you prefer a bit of a kick on flavour.

If you want to serve them to younger babies, fry over a low heat for a softer texture. Don't forget to serve some of the veggies on the side too!

9+ MONTHS

Courgette Fritters

PREP: 10 minutes
COOK: 5 minutes

SERVES: 2 PEOPLE (MAKES 8–10 FRITTERS)

- 1 courgette, grated
- 1 egg, beaten
- 3 tbsp chickpea flour (also known as gram flour or 'besan'), or plain flour
- 40g cheddar cheese, grated
- handful of finely chopped fresh parsley
- olive oil, for drizzling

OPTIONAL SPICES
- ½ tsp ground cumin
- ½ tsp ground black pepper
- ½ tsp mild sweet paprika

Put the grated courgette in a clean cloth or tea towel and squeeze to remove excess liquid. Transfer the courgette to a mixing bowl and add the egg, flour, cheese, parsley and spices and mix until well combined.

Heat a generous amount of olive oil in a frying pan over a medium-high heat. Use a large spoon or ice-cream scoop to carefully place piles of the mixture in the pan and fry for 5 minutes, flattening them while they cook and flipping them to ensure they are cooked all the way through and have a crispy texture.

Remove from the pan, leave to cool a little, then serve.

two

8+ MONTHS

Carrot Fritters

PREP: 10 minutes
COOK: 5 minutes

SERVES: 2 PEOPLE (MAKES 12–14 FRITTERS)

- 1 carrot, finely grated
- 1 egg, beaten
- 40g cheddar cheese, grated
- handful of chives, finely chopped (optional)
- 3 tbsp chickpea flour (also known as gram flour or 'besan'), or plain flour
- olive oil, for drizzling

Put the grated carrot, egg, cheese and chives (if using) in a bowl with the flour and mix until well combined.

Heat a generous amount of olive oil in a frying pan over a medium-high heat. Use a large spoon or ice-cream scoop to carefully place 8–10 piles of the mixture in the pan and fry for 5 minutes, flattening them while they cook and flipping them to ensure they are cooked all the way through and have a crispy texture.

Remove from the pan, leave to cool a little, then serve.

Tip
If your baby is at the start of weaning, you can steam the grated carrot first to make it softer.

7+ MONTHS

Corn Fritters

three

PREP: 10 minutes
COOK: 5 minutes

SERVES: 2 PEOPLE (MAKES 8–10 FRITTERS)

- 160g tinned sweetcorn, drained and squished a little
- 1 egg, beaten
- ½ tsp baking powder
- 50ml milk of choice
- handful of finely chopped fresh coriander (optional)
- 3 tbsp chickpea flour (also known as gram flour or 'besan'), or plain flour
- olive oil, for drizzling

Put the sweetcorn, egg, baking powder, milk and coriander (if using) in a blender with the flour then blend the mixture.

Heat a generous amount of olive oil in a frying pan over a medium-high heat. Use a large spoon or ice-cream scoop to carefully place piles of the mixture in the pan and fry for 5 minutes, flattening them while they cook and flipping them to ensure they are cooked all the way through and have a crispy texture.

Remove from the pan, leave to cool a little, then serve.

6+ MONTHS

No-bowl Veggie Egg Muffins

If you're looking for light and fluffy egg bites which are prepared directly in the muffin tin (yes that's right – nothing to wash up!) and still packed with veggies, then this right here is for you. You can divide a muffin into quarters and confidently know that your baby has eaten a whole egg over the course of a few days.

PREP: 5 minutes
COOK: 20 minutes

MAKES: 6 MUFFINS

- 6 medium eggs
- small handful of chopped spinach
- 1 plum tomato, finely chopped
- 1 tsp dried mixed herbs
- 25–30g cheddar cheese, grated (optional)

Preheat the oven to 190°C and grease 6 holes of a muffin tin generously with olive oil or line it with baking paper.

Crack an egg into each muffin hole, then add all the other ingredients except the cheese, dividing them evenly among the holes. Stir gently with a spoon to break the yolk, then sprinkle cheese on top.

Bake in the oven for 17–20 minutes, until the egg is set and the cheese bubbling.

Remove from the oven and leave to cool, then remove from the tin.

Swap
- Feel free to substitute the veg above for whatever you have to hand, such as grated carrot or courgette.

11+ MONTHS

Carrot Cake Oat Bars

I know we are not supposed to have favourites but these are always a big hit with my toddler and myself, as they are infused with all the flavours of carrot cake and sweetened with dates which creates a lovely moist, sticky texture that leaves you wanting more! If you make them regularly, you may wish to leave out the dates to avoid your baby acquiring a sweet-preference.

PREP: 10 minutes
COOK: 35 minutes

MAKES: 10–12 BARS

- 5–6 dried dates
- 2 ripe bananas, peeled
- 120g rolled oats
- 30g smooth almond butter, plus extra to serve
- 120ml milk of choice
- 1 tsp ground cinnamon
- ½ carrot, peeled and grated

Preheat the oven to 180°C and line a roughly 21cm baking dish with baking paper.

To soften the dates, put them in a heatproof bowl, cover with hot water and leave them to soak for 5 minutes until soft, then drain and chop or mash them, keeping 2 tablespoons of the date soaking water.

Mash the bananas in a bowl until smooth and stir in the oats, almond butter, milk and cinnamon and fold in the grated carrot and chopped or mashed dates. Add 2 tablespoons of the leftover date soaking water to loosen the mix if needed.

Pour the mixture into the baking dish and smooth it out with a spoon or fork, then bake for 35 minutes, until golden and well baked.

Remove from the oven and leave to cool for 5–10 minutes before cutting into bars. Serve with a cream cheese topping for the win or leave it as is!

Tip
To loosen the cream cheese and give it a runnier consistency, add a splash of milk and whisk together then spread it on top. Icing sugar can be added for grown-ups.

Peanut Butter Cookies

12+ MONTHS

These cookies are a firm favourite for toddler snacks. We made them non-stop in our house for a post-nursery 'pick-me-up' and I've found they are a great way to involve your toddler with baking as there are only four simple ingredients. The cookies are egg free, dairy free and wheat free, with no refined sugars.

PREP: 25 minutes
COOK: 10–12 minutes

MAKES: 8–10 COOKIES

- 2 ripe bananas, peeled
- 130g smooth peanut butter
- 200g rolled oats
- 50g raspberries
- 25g chocolate chips (optional)

Preheat the oven to 190°C and line a baking tray with baking parchment.

Mash the bananas in a bowl then stir in the peanut butter, followed by the oats. Stir to form a dough, then fold in the raspberries and chocolate chips (if using).

Divide the mixture into 8–10 equal pieces, place them on the lined baking tray and flatten them down to a cookie shape (the cookies will hold this shape as they cook).

Bake in the oven for 12 minutes, until golden, then remove, leave to cool on the tray and enjoy! Try not to overbake them as this will give the cookies a firmer texture, and you want them softer for babies.

Tip
Add choc chips for grown-ups and older children – they work perfectly.

11+ MONTHS

Sweet Potato Crackers

This four-ingredient snack is so moreish that my husband and I had to separate out our kids' portions as we were completely addicted!

PREP: 30 minutes
COOK: 15–20 minutes

SERVES: 4 PEOPLE

- 200g plain flour, plus extra for dusting
- 1 tsp baking powder
- 250g cooked sweet potato
- 65g unsalted butter, melted
- super-green hummus, to serve (page 240)

Preheat the oven to 180°C and line a baking tray with baking paper.

Mix the flour and baking powder in a bowl, then add the cooked sweet potato and melted butter and mix with your hands until it comes together to form a dough.

Roll out the dough to a thickness of 5mm (if it sticks, dust the surface with flour), then cut it into squares and place them on the lined baking tray, re-rolling any leftover dough.

Bake for 10–12 minutes, until they are lightly golden. For younger babies, take them out of the oven 1–2 minutes early, so they are not too hard.

Remove from the oven and leave to cool.

Dip into hummus and serve to your baby.

Tip
The crackers will keep well for 2–3 days in an airtight container.

SNACKS AND DIPS

6+ MONTHS

Raita – Three Ways

This yoghurt-based dish is a great source of protein, carbohydrate and fat and is also rich in calcium to help support healthy bone development. Served traditionally alongside curries, it has a cooling effect which also makes it a handy teething remedy. It works best with my kitcheri recipe (page 130), tandoori chicken (page 268) and lentil fritters (page 176) too. Use plant-based/soya yoghurt if you prefer.

---

one

Cucumber Raita

PREP: 5 minutes

SERVES: 1 ADULT AND 1 CHILD

- 150g plain natural yoghurt
- ½ cucumber, peeled
- handful of mint leaves, finely chopped (optional)

Put the yoghurt in a bowl, grate in the cucumber and stir. Add the mint (if using) and serve.

two

Ginger and Lemon Raita

PREP: 5 minutes

SERVES: 1 ADULT AND 1 CHILD

- 150g plain natural yoghurt
- juice of ½ lemon
- 1cm piece of ginger, finely grated

Put the yoghurt in a bowl with the lemon juice and stir. Add the ginger and serve.

three

Tomato and Cumin Raita

PREP: 5 minutes

SERVES: 1 ADULT AND 1 CHILD

- 150g plain natural yoghurt
- 4 cherry tomatoes
- ½ tsp ground cumin
- handful of fresh coriander (optional)

Put all the ingredients in a blender and blend until smooth. Transfer to a bowl and serve.

Tip
We tend to use natural yoghurt for raita to create the best texture and flavour while also containing natural gut-friendly bacteria to support the immune system.

6+ MONTHS

Super-green Hummus

This is a great way to use up any leftover cooked greens or fresh herbs – it just all goes straight into the blender for ease.

PREP: 10 minutes

SERVES: 2 ADULTS AND 2 CHILDREN

- 1 ripe avocado, halved, stoned and peeled
- 400g tin chickpeas, drained and rinsed
- large handful of spinach
- handful of fresh coriander
- handful of fresh parsley
- juice of ½ lemon, plus extra to taste
- 2 tbsp olive oil
- 1 tbsp tahini

Put all the ingredients in a blender and blend until smooth. Taste and add more lemon juice for an extra kick.

Serve with toast fingers or as a dip for veggie sticks or with my Sweet Potato Crackers (page 236).

SNACKS AND DIPS

6+ MONTHS

Cuca-mole

This guacamole has a little twist with the addition of grated cucumber which makes it super refreshing.

PREP: 10 minutes

SERVES: 2–3 PEOPLE

- 2 large avocados, halved, stoned and peeled
- juice of ½ lime
- ½ tsp mild sweet paprika
- ⅓ cucumber, grated
- handful of chopped fresh coriander

Use the back of a fork to mash the avocado flesh in a bowl until smooth. Add the lime juice and paprika, then the cucumber and coriander, and mix to combine.

Serve with toast or pitta fingers – it makes a great snack.

Tip
When you buy avocados, pick the nub of the stem off the top to see if it is green underneath which will indicate it is perfectly ripe. If it is a light green colour, it is likely not ripe enough and if it is a brown colour, then it is likely the avocado is overripe.

6+ MONTHS

Creamy Butter Bean Dip

Butter beans are a great source of fibre, protein, iron and folate, which help support your baby's digestive system, muscles and brain development respectively. Serving them as a dip makes it a little more interesting to your baby and gives you an opportunity to add some flavour with garlic. Butter beans can also be blended into sauces to boost nutrient intake.

PREP: 10 minutes

SERVES: 2 ADULTS AND 2 CHILDREN

- 400g tin butter beans, drained and rinsed
- 1 small garlic clove
- 2 tbsp full-fat unsweetened Greek yoghurt
- 3 tbsp olive oil

Put all the ingredients in a blender and blend until smooth, loosen the mixture with a splash of water if needed.

Serve with veggies or toast fingers.

Tip
If you want the dip to have a smoother consistency, add more olive oil. This will also increase the fat content for baby – remember, healthy fats are unrestricted until the age of two.

6+ MONTHS

Smashed Peas

If you're worried about peas being a choking hazard, but still want to serve this nutrient-rich, high protein veggie, then try this smashed pea recipe (it's great with my fishcakes on page 194).

PREP: 10 minutes

SERVES: 2 ADULTS AND 2 CHILDREN

- 300g frozen peas, cooked
- 1 or 2 garlic cloves (I use 2 but you may want to start with 1)
- small handful of fresh mint leaves
- juice of ½ lime (lemon will also do!)
- 3 tbsp olive oil
- 1 tbsp tahini (optional, for extra smoothness and sesame exposure)

Put all the ingredients in a blender and blend until smooth. Serve on crusty bread drizzled with olive oil. Add salt and chilli flakes for grown-ups!

Tip
The crusty part of the bread can help your baby with exploring different areas of their mouth and strengthening those jaw muscles.

6+ MONTHS

Chia Jam – Three Ways

What I love about chia jam is that you can make it at home for you and your baby with only two simple ingredients, without needing to add any refined sugar or preservatives.

Serve these fruit chia jams on toast fingers or simply with natural yoghurt as a pudding. Ensure the berries are ripe for best results. The jams will keep for up to one week in the fridge.

---

one

Raspberry Chia Jam

PREP: 5 minutes

SERVES: 2 ADULTS AND 2 CHILDREN

- 150g raspberries
- 2 tsp chia seeds

Mash the raspberries in a microwaveable bowl with a fork and microwave for 90–120 seconds until slightly bubbling. Add the chia seeds and mash further if needed. Leave to cool and thicken for at least 10 minutes, then serve.

continued overleaf...

two

Blueberry Chia Jam

PREP: 5 minutes

SERVES: 2 ADULTS AND 2 CHILDREN

- 150g blueberries
- 2 tsp chia seeds

Mash the blueberries in a microwaveable bowl with a fork and microwave for 90–120 seconds until slightly bubbling. Add the chia seeds and mash further if needed. Leave to cool and thicken for at least 10 minutes, then serve.

three

Strawberry Chia Jam

PREP: 5 minutes

SERVES: 2 ADULTS AND 2 CHILDREN

- 150g strawberries, hulled
- 2 tsp chia seeds

Mash the strawberries in a microwaveable bowl with a fork and microwave for 90–120 seconds until slightly bubbling. Mash with a fork into a pulp, microwave for a further minute then add the chia seeds. Leave to cool and thicken for at least 10 minutes, then serve. Pass the pulp through a sieve for younger babies (<9 months) to result in a smoother consistency, if needed.

SNACKS AND DIPS

Conversion tables

WEIGHTS *

METRIC	IMPERIAL
15 g	1/2 oz
25 g	1 oz
40 g	1½ oz
50 g	2 oz
75 g	3 oz
100 g	4 oz
150 g	5 oz
175 g	6 oz
200 g	7 oz
225 g	8 oz
250 g	9 oz
275 g	10 oz
350 g	12 oz
375 g	13 oz
400 g	14 oz
425 g	15 oz
450 g	1 lb
550 g	1¼ lb
675 g	1½ lb
900 g	2 lb
1.5 kg	3 lb
1.75 kg	4 lb
2.25 kg	5 lb

* 28.35g = 1oz but the measurements here have been rounded up or down to make conversion easier

VOLUME

METRIC	IMPERIAL
25 ml	1 fl oz
50 ml	2 fl oz
85 ml	3 fl oz
150 ml	5 fl oz (¼ pint)
300 ml	10 fl oz (¼ pint)
450 ml	15 fl oz (¾ pint)
600 ml	1 pint
700 ml	1¼ pints
900 ml	1½ pints
1 litre	1¾ pints
1.2 litres	2 pints
1.25 litres	2¼ pints
1.5 litres	2½ pints
1.6 litres	2¾ pints
1.75 litres	3 pints
1.8 litres	3¼ pints
2 litres	3½ pints
2.1 litres	3¾ pints
2.25 litres	4 pints
2.75 litres	5 pints
3.4 litres	6 pints
3.9 litres	7 pints
5 litres	8 pints (1 gal)

CONVERSION CHARTS

MEASUREMENTS

METRIC	IMPERIAL
0.5 cm	¼ inch
1 cm	½ inch
2.5 cm	1 inch
5 cm	2 inches
7.5 cm	3 inches
10 cm	4 inches
15 cm	6 inches
18 cm	7 inches
20 cm	8 inches
23 cm	9 inches
25 cm	10 inches
30 cm	12 inches

OVEN TEMPERATURES

°C	°F	GAS MK
140°C	275°F	Gas Mk 1
150°C	300°F	Gas Mk 2
160°C	325°F	Gas Mk 3
180°C	350°F	Gas Mk 4
190°C	375°F	Gas Mk 5
200°C	400°F	Gas Mk 6
220°C	425°F	Gas Mk 7
230°C	450°F	Gas Mk 8
240°C	475°F	Gas Mk 9

Useful resources

Allergy UK
Allergy Resources
Helpline: 01322 619898
Website: www.allergyuk.org

Anaphylaxis UK
Allergy factsheets
Website: www.anaphylaxis.org.uk

Bliss baby charity
For babies born premature or sick
Website: www.bliss.org.uk

Breastfeeding Network
Breastfeeding support
Website: www.breastfeedingnetwork.org.uk

British Nutrition Foundation
Nutrition for babies, toddlers and preschoolers, and portion guides
Website: www.nutrition.org.uk

British Society for Allergy and Clinical Immunology (BCASI)
Practical advice on preventing allergy in your baby
Website: www.bsaci.org/wp-content/uploads/2020/02/pdf_Infant-feeding-and-allergy-prevention-PARENTS-FINAL-booklet.pdf

First 1000 days
Why 1000 days
Website: thousanddays.org

First Steps Nutrition Trust
Eating Well Resources
Website: www.firststepsnutrition.org/eating-well-early-years

GP Infant Feeding Network
Milk Allergy in Primary Care Guideline
Website: gpifn.org.uk/imap

La Leche League
Breastfeeding support
Helpline: 0345 1202918
Website: laleche.org.uk

NHS Start for Life
Introducing your baby to solids
Website: www.nhs.uk/start-for-life/baby/weaning

National Institute of Care Excellence (NICE)
Clinical Knowledge Summaries (CKS) – Health topics
Website: cks.nice.org.uk/topics

Royal College of Paediatrics and Child Health (RCPCH)
Growth charts
Website: www.rcpch.ac.uk/resources/uk-who-growth-charts-0-4-years

World Health Organisation
Infant feeding
Website: www.who.int/news-room/factsheets/detail/infant-and-young-child-feeding

For more advice on feeding your child, health tips and family recipes, follow my Instagram account: @theweaninggp

Endnotes

Chapter 1

There is a growing body of research to suggest that the first 1,000 days of your child's life can have lifelong consequences on their health and well-being. (page 28)
thousanddays.org/why-1000-days/building-brains

I have included a table below listing all eight B vitamins with good food sources and the individual roles they play within our bodies. (page 36)
www.nhs.uk/conditions/vitamins-and-minerals/vitamin-b/

There are lots of benefits to consuming a more plant-based diet, with many studies in adults showing a reduced risk of developing long-term diseases such as heart disease, high blood pressure and obesity. (page 42)
pubmed.ncbi.nlm.nih.gov/30828449/
pubmed.ncbi.nlm.nih.gov/23364007/

Common choking hazards (page 46)
www.cdc.gov/infant-toddler-nutrition/foods-and-drinks/choking-hazards.html

There is some research to suggest that excessive salt in childhood could potentially increase the risk of high blood pressure in later life, although much more research and controlled studies in humans are needed. (page 48)
www.actiononsalt.org.uk/salthealth/salt-and-children

Advice has now changed about how to introduce allergens to babies following two major studies (LEAP and EAT). (page 54)
pmc.ncbi.nlm.nih.gov/articles/PMC4852987/
www.nejm.org/doi/full/10.1056/NEJMoa1414850

Interestingly, a recent follow-up study has shown that children who had consumed regular, frequent peanut until the age of five still had a reduced risk of developing a peanut allergy in adolescence regardless of how much peanut was consumed after the age of five. (page 54)
evidence.nejm.org/doi/full/10.1056/EVIDoa2300311

The EAT study showed that babies who were introduced to wheat in the four- to six-month window were less likely to develop coeliac disease at the age of three, but this study only looked at breastfed babies and there is very limited information on this topic. (page 62)
pubmed.ncbi.nlm.nih.gov/32986087/

Immediate and delayed type food allergy (page 58-59)
www.bsaci.org/wp-content/uploads/2020/02/pdf_Early-feeding-guidance-for-HCPs-2.pdf

Chapter 2

There is some research to suggest that introducing bitter flavours such as vegetables early on when starting solids and consistently exposing your baby to them can increase their acceptance of vegetables until at least 12 months, and potentially thereafter. (page 71)
pmc.ncbi.nlm.nih.gov/articles/PMC9174121/

Even on a hot day, studies have shown that breastfed babies do not need any extra fluids but may naturally breastfeed more frequently if needed. (page 77)
pmc.ncbi.nlm.nih.gov/articles/PMC9485728/

The British Society of Paediatric Dentistry and NHS guidance recommend starting with an open cup as it helps to teach a baby how to sip rather than suck from an early age. (page 92)
543dentalcentre.co.uk/wp-content/uploads/2018/10/BSPD-Practical-parenting-guide.pdf

Introducing cutlery timeline (page 94-95)
www.nhsggc.org.uk/media/272346/using-cutlery-information-sheet.pdf

The current thresholds for 'faltering growth' are... (page 106)
cks.nice.org.uk/topics/faltering-growth/

Managing Your Own Anxieties (page 110)
www.allergyuk.org/wp-content/uploads/2021/08/Coping-with-Anxiety.pdf

Acknowledgements

I would like to say a huge thank you to every single one of my followers who have become part of our growing online community over the last three years. Without your continuing support, questions and time spent making our recipes, this book would not have been created.

I would like to extend this thank you to my literary agent Jonathan Conway for his calm reassurance, my publisher Ebury at Penguin Random House and editorial director Samantha Jackson for giving me this opportunity. A further thank you to my editor Leah Feltham, who I have worked with closely throughout this process, for her constant guidance, dedication and hard work to bring this book to fruition. A special mention to my editorial consultant Julia Kellaway for her non-judgmental and efficient feedback of what I like to call 'my ramble on a page.' A big thank you to the incredibly talented Claire Winfield and Maud Eden for producing the food photography – this was a once in a lifetime experience that I will never forget.

I am grateful to Professor Adam Fox (Consultant Paediatric Allergy Specialist) for his review of the allergy section to ensure the most up-to-date information is shared here. I am further delighted to have had the well-known and highly respected Dr Amir Khan (GP) reviewing the general medical information. I am extremely fortunate to have the specialist review of paediatric dietitian and child nutrition expert, Paula Hallam, NHS advanced paediatric dietitian Charlotte Ockleton, NHS advanced paediatric and neonatal dietitian Siyma Hussain, NHS advanced practitioner neonatal speech and language therapist Rachel Evans and NHS Consultant paediatric dentist Srishti Datta. The time, advice and kindness you have all shown has been invaluable.

I could not have written this book without the unwavering support and commitment of my husband, Varun, who has always been the backbone of The Weaning GP. It was Varun who insisted I start my Instagram page after seeing how fixated I was about educating others and sharing recipes amongst our friends and family. I am eternally indebted to you and our two children, without whom I would not have experienced our weaning journey, learnt so much, or had 24/7 food tasters for my recipes!

And of course, to our dear family and friends – thank you for your encouragement, positivity and inspiration along the way. In particular, to the South-Asian women in my life who have cooked for us and continue to cook for us now – you have been influential in my creation of wholesome and flavoursome recipes.

Finally, to the parents and caregivers who are reading this, I am so appreciative for entrusting me to join you on your unique weaning journey and allowing our recipes to enter your home.

I hope this book is everything you were searching for and more.

Best wishes,

Sarika x

Index

allergens 52–3, 56, 84–7, 117, 121
allergies 53–63, 84–7
anaemia, iron-deficiency 33
anatomical differences 18
anxieties, parental 110–12
apple
  apple crumble 218
  apple oat bars 228
avocado
  avo-banana pancakes 127
  avocado and egg toast 142
  chicken and avo fusilli 137
  cuca-mole 241

balanced meals 27–43
banana
  avo-banana pancakes 127
  banana bread 221
  French toast 173
  smoothie bowl 163
bean(s)
  butter bean dip 242
  kidney bean curry 193
  masala beans 175
  quesadillas 178
  sweet potato and black bean mash 135
berry crumble 218
blondie 220
blueberry
  blueberry chia jam 246
  blueberry scones 159
breakfast 140–63
breastfeeding 10, 26, 77, 98–9
broccoli omelette strips 138

cakes
  baby cake slice 216
  banana bread 221
  blondies 220
  carrot cake oat bars 233
calcium 40–1
carbohydrates 29
carrot
  carrot cake oat bars 233
  carrot fritters 230
  carrot pudding 222
cauliflower potato tots 226

cheese
  mac 'n' cheese 203
  unpasteurised 50
cheesecakes, mini oat 215
chia jam 245–6
chicken
  butter chicken curry 188
  chicken and avo fusilli 137
  chicken fajita 195
  tandoori-style drumsticks 168
  veg, tofu and chicken curry 207
choking 44–7
cod, curried rice 206
coeliac disease 62
combination feeding 23, 24
constipation 108–9
contact reactions 60
cookies, peanut butter 235
cooling food 101
cottage cheese, scrambled 183
courgette fritters 229
cow's milk 86–7
  transition to 43, 98–9
cow's milk protein allergy (CMPA) 61
crackers, sweet potato 236
cream cheese
  cream cheese and cucumber toast 143
  French toast 173
crêpes, lentil 147
crumble 217–18
cucumber
  cream cheese and cucumber toast 143
  cuca-mole 241
  cucumber raita 237
cups 92–3, 101, 117
curry
  butter chicken 188
  curried cod rice 206
  kidney bean 193
  saag tofu vegan 200
  spiced vegetables 131
  veg, tofu and chicken 207
cutlery, introduction 94–5

defrosting food 101
dental care 49
development 10, 12–16, 19
developmental delays 18
dinners 186–209
dips 224–47

eating out 96–7
eczema 54–6, 58–9
egg 86–7
  egg and avo toast 142
  omelettes 138, 150
  raw 50
  veggie egg muffins 232
equipment 66–8

fajita, chicken 195
fats and oils 30, 42
finger foods 22–4, 45, 80
first 1,000 days 28
first tastes 71
fish 51, 86–7
  curried cod rice 206
  salmon, broccoli and potato 128
  salmon fishcakes 194
  salmon poke bowl 166
  tuna jackets 134
flatbread, lentil/potato 176
food on-the-go 101
food preparation 100
food protein-induced enterocolitis syndrome (FPIES) 62
food safety/storage 100–1
food texture 78–9
food variety 30–1, 91, 117
foods to avoid 48–51
formula feeding 10, 26, 98–9
French toast 171–3
frittata, four-veg 129
fritters — three ways 229–30
fullness cues 74, 88

gagging 44–5
genetic differences 18
growth, faltering 17, 105–6

herbs 120

high-calorie diets 107
honey 48
hummus, super-green 240
hunger cues 74, 88
hygiene 101

illness 103–5
iodine 38
iron 32–3, 42, 116

jackets, tuna 134
jam, chia 245–6

lactose intolerance 61
lasagne, one-pot 198
lassi, mango 162
lentil(s)
   lentil crêpes 147
   lentil flatbread 176
   lentil rice 130
   lentil soup 184
loaf, rise and shine 153
lunches 164–84

macronutrients 29–31
mango lassi 162
marinades 168, 188
mash 135
mealtimes 88–97
messy babies 88, 91, 117
metabolic disorders 18
micronutrients 32–42
milk 26, 43, 51, 77
see also cow's milk
minerals 32–3, 38–41, 42
muffins
   fruity 149
   veggie egg 232
   veggie-loaded 177
   Weetabix 152
multiples (babies) 17

neurological conditions 18
noodles, satay 204
nut milks 43
nuts 50, 86–7
   overnight oats 146

oat(s)
   apple oat bars 228
   carrot cake oat bars 233
   mini oat cheesecakes 215

overnight oats 146
omelette
   broccoli 138
   green masala 150

pancakes
   mini avo-banana 127
   vegan 182
parental anxieties 110–12
pasta
   chicken and avocado 137
   mac 'n' cheese 203
   one-pot lasagne 198
   orzo soup 184
   pistachio pesto 180
   prawn 208
   sweetcorn 174
   veggie 192
peanut(s) 50, 86–7
   peanut butter cookies 235
   peanut butter French toast 173
   smoothie bowl 163
pear and ginger crumble 217
pea(s), smashed 243
pistachio pesto pasta 180
pizza
   pizza French toast 172
   sweet potato pizzas 191
plant-based diets 42, 182, 200
porridge
   golden 156
   spiced orange 124
portion sizes 73–6
potato
   cauliflower potato tots 226
   flatbread 176
   tuna jackets 134
pouches 79
prawn
   linguine 208
   satay noodles 204
premature babies 18
professional help 18–19, 112
protein 29, 42, 46
puddings 210–23

quesadillas 178

raita 237
raspberry
   blondies 220

chia jam 143, 245
   overnight oats 146
reheating food 101
rice
   curried cod 206
   lentil 130
   rice pudding 212
rice milk 51

salmon
   salmon, broccoli and potato 128
   salmon fishcakes 194
   salmon poke bowl 166
salt 48
scones, blueberry 159
sensitive gag reflex 105
serving food 100
sesame allergies 86–7
shellfish 51, 86–7
slushies 51
smoothie bowls 161–3
snacks 17, 81, 224–47
soup 184
soy 86–7
spices 120
spinach and tofu curry 200
spoon-feeding 21, 23, 24
storage advice 120
strawberry
   French toast 173
   strawberry chia jam 246
sugar 48–9
sweet potato
   sweet potato crackers 236
   sweet potato mash 135
   sweet potato pizzas 191
   sweet potato quesadillas 178
sweetcorn
   corn fritters 230
   sweetcorn tagliatelle 174

teething 102–3
textures (food) 78–9
toast 142–3, 171–3
tofu
   saag tofu curry 200
   veg, tofu and chicken curry 207
tomato and cumin raita 237
tongue tie (ankyloglossia) 105

transition meals 119, 122–39
tuna jackets 134

vegan diets 42, 182, 200
vegetables
　how to serve 72
　spiced 131
vegetarian diets 42
vitamins 32–8, 42

water intake 77
weaning
　baby-led 22–4, 116
　definition 10
　getting started 65–117
　handling setbacks 102–9
　how to 20–6
　mantras 113
　principles 7, 9–63, 116–17
　reasons for 10
　recipes 122–247
　schedules 82–3
　signs of readiness 16–19
　slow to wean babies 104
　things to watch out for 44–51
　and time of day 70
　when to start 12–15
weetabix smoothie bowl 162
wheat allergy 62, 86–7

yoghurt and jam toast 142

zinc 38, 42

Dr Sarika Dewan is an NHS GP with an advanced knowledge of women's healthcare. When she encountered multiple challenges weaning her first baby, including a traumatic choking incident, she struggled to find evidence-based, practical resources to guide her. Instead, to alleviate her anxiety and rebuild her confidence, she researched everything possible about weaning. Combining this with her existing medical experience empowered her to embrace the weaning journey. As The Weaning GP on Instagram (@theweaninggp), Sarika is passionate about helping other parents. She is the only UK doctor on social media solely talking about weaning, and has built a strong and engaged online community.

VERMILION

UK | USA | Canada | Ireland | Australia
India | New Zealand | South Africa

Vermilion is part of the Penguin Random House group of companies whose addresses can be found at global.penguinrandomhouse.com

Penguin Random House UK
One Embassy Gardens, 8 Viaduct Gardens, London SW11 7BW

penguin.co.uk
global.penguinrandomhouse.com

First published by Vermilion in 2025

1

Copyright © Dr Sarika Dewan 2025
Photography © Clare Winfield 2025
Illustrations pages 4, 8, 12–13, 15, 29, 30, 33, 37, 40, 46, 48, 49, 51, 56, 66, 72, 80, 85, 90, 96, 97, 100, 101, 108, 118, 122, 119, 163 © Alyona; Al Rafi; Ewelina; FyfaMetarial; Good studio; GreenSkyStudio; Hilda; Ira; Karolna; Lil_22; Lynea; Marina; Motsuniko; Radoma; Rinrin; Shahida; Sunnydream – stock.adobe.com
Illustrations from www.flaticon.com (thermometer image page 85 adapted from icon by Dinosoft; slushie and swordfish icons page 51, bread icon page 56, baby cup icon page 67, sippy cup icons pages 93 and 101 all made by Freepik; hazelnut icon page 46 made by Manshagraphic; soy icon page 87 by Max. Icons; bread icon page 56 made by Meaicon; defrosting icon page 101 by Smashicons)
Minced avocado photograph page 78 © Fotema/Shutterstock
Cutlery by Pippeta

The moral right of the author has been asserted.

Penguin Random House values and supports copyright. Copyright fuels creativity, encourages diverse voices, promotes freedom of expression and supports a vibrant culture. Thank you for purchasing an authorised edition of this book and for respecting intellectual property laws by not reproducing, scanning or distributing any part of it by any means without permission. You are supporting authors and enabling Penguin Random House to continue to publish books for everyone. No part of this book may be used or reproduced in any manner for the purpose of training artificial intelligence technologies or systems. In accordance with Article 4(3) of the DSM Directive 2019/790, Penguin Random House expressly reserves this work from the text and data mining exception.

Editorial Director: Sam Jackson
Editor: Leah Feltham
Assistant Editor: Sonam Nundoochan
Copyeditors: Julia Kellaway and Laura Nickoll
Production: Lucy Harrison
Designer: maru studio G.K.
Photographer: Clare Winfield
Food Stylist: Maud Eden
Prop Stylist: Hannah Wilkinson

Colour origination by Altaimage Ltd
Printed and bound in China by C & C Offset Printing Co., Ltd

The authorised representative in the EEA is Penguin Random House Ireland, Morrison Chambers, 32 Nassau Street, Dublin D02 YH68.

A CIP catalogue record for this book is available from the British Library.

ISBN 9781785045400

Penguin Random House is committed to a sustainable future for our business, our readers and our planet. This book is made from Forest Stewardship Council® certified paper.